ELT Review
General Editor: Chris Kennedy

Young Learners of English: Some Research Perspectives

Editor:
SHELAGH RIXON
University of Warwick

Pearson Education Limited
Edinburgh Gate, Harlow
Essex CM20 2JE, England

Series concept and name © The British Council
(registered charity number 209131)

Text © Pearson Education Limited 1999

All rights reserved; no part of this publication may be reproduced, stored in any
retrieval system, or transmitted in any form or by any means, electronic, mechanical,
photocopying, recording, or otherwise without either the prior written permission of the
Publishers or a licence permitting restricted copying in the United Kingdom issued by
the Copyright Licensing Agency Ltd., 90 Tottenham Court Road, London W1P 9HE

ISBN 0 582 42082 2

Set in ITC Century
Packaged by Aldridge Press
Produced by Pearson Education Limited
Printed and bound in United Kingdom by Redvine

Acknowledgements: The editor and Publishers acknowledge with thanks
the following copyright material reproduced in this book:
Adaptation of *Granny Sticklebeck* by J. Moore and M. Wright, Hamish Hamilton 1981;
How Does a Czar Eat Potatoes? by A. Rose, Abelard-Schuman; the poem 'Poor Pussy'
from *The Flying Cow*, Interpress Publishers, Warsaw 1988; two pages from *The Tales of
a Furry Friend*, Ion Creanga Publishing House 1977; page from *Die Ampel*
Ravensburger Buchverlags Otto Maier GmbH 1987

The publishers wish to state that they have made every effort to trace the copyright
holders, but if they have inadvertently overlooked any they will be pleased to make the
necessary arrangements at the first opportunity.

Correspondence on editorial matters and proposals for the series should be sent to:
Chris Kennedy
Centre for English Language Studies, University of Birmingham
Westmere, Edgbaston Park Road, BIRMINGHAM B15 2TT, UK
(Tel: 0121 414 5695/6; Fax: 0121 414 3298; e-mail c.j.kennedy@bham.ac.uk)

Contents

	Introduction SHELAGH RIXON	v
1	**Investigations into Task-related Strategy Use with Young Learners of English** ANNAMARIA PINTER	1
2	**Teaching Vocabulary Through Rhythmic Refrains in Stories** HAVOVI KOLSAWALLA	18
3	**The Value of Grammatical Information in a Dictionary for Young Learners** HILARY NESI	32
4	**Enchantment in the Classroom: Children's Literature as a Teaching Aid** PIOTR KUHIWCZAK	43
5	**Where Do the Words in EYL Textbooks Come From?** SHELAGH RIXON	55
6	**'Natural Born Speakers of English': Code Switching in Pair- and Group-work in Hungarian Primary Classrooms** MARIANNE NIKOLOV	72
7	**Assessment of Young Learners' English: Reasons and Means** PAULINE REA-DICKINS AND SHELAGH RIXON	89
	Statistical Procedures	102
	Bibliography	104

Introduction

Shelagh Rixon
Centre for English Language Teacher Education
University of Warwick

This volume of English Language Teaching Review concerns the teaching of English to Young Learners (EYL), and in particular it focuses on different types of research that are currently being undertaken to illuminate classroom practice. The focus is therefore on instructional situations rather than on situations in which the language is acquired through exposure to it outside school. The aim is to present findings and discussions that may be interesting in themselves to teachers and trainers from a wide variety of Young Learner teaching situations, but also to illustrate research procedures that can be replicated by readers who wish to investigate similar issues in their own environments.

Some definitions of terms

Young Learners

The definition of Young Learners (YL) for our purposes is children between the ages of about 5 years old to 12 years old. In the British educational system, and those in many other countries, this corresponds roughly with the years spent in the primary or elementary stages of formal education before the transition to secondary school. The upper age limit is a convenient one since in many other countries, too, the age of 11 or 12 brings a change from one type of school to a different one, or from one department to another within a single institution. It is also true that, in the experience of many teachers, children at about the age of 11 or 12 begin to change in their approaches to many aspects of life and learning, including the learning of a foreign language.

Psycholinguists and psychologists have for many years tried to trace the development of children's capacities for, and approaches to, language learning. However, it is not the purpose of this volume to develop further the seemingly perennial discussion of whether there is an optimum age for language learning, and whether it is true that children below the age of puberty have special faculties which cannot be tapped after this developmental stage. In support of the more concrete approach of this volume it seems worthwhile to make two points:

- The first is that the optimal age is not a concept that can ever apply in a vacuum. It makes more sense to think in terms of optimal conditions, which may include age as one factor, but must also include the circumstances in which the learners find themselves, the role of the new language in the society as a whole, the quality and quantity of input to which they are exposed and the chances that are available for the learners to make real use of the language they are learning.

- The second is that decisions in many countries about the appropriateness of introducing English to Young Learners often seem to be made at a level which is more likely to be driven by political and economic ambitions, and may not involve deep consideration either of the research on language-learning capacities at different ages, or of optimum conditions. The reasons may include a quasi-symbolic rejection of another language (for example Russian in some former Soviet bloc countries), a faith that providing a longer exposure to the foreign language by lowering the starting age may solve problems of low achievement in the secondary school, or a view of foreign-language learning at an early age as one way of broadening children's cultural horizons and breaking down any tendency to insularity or prejudice. To these may be added the ever vigorous influence of parents, for many of whom the provision of English in schools is seen as vital for giving their children a better chance for the future. For further discussion of these issues see Rixon (1992).

Thus, whatever the future verdict of research on whether Young Learners are psycholinguistically 'specially gifted' in some ways, we are faced with a situation world-wide in which Young Learners are seen by administrators and educationalists as worth treating as special while the jury is still out. A survey undertaken in late 1998 for the British Council (The British Council and Rixon, 1999) revealed that teaching English to Young Learners, started in many countries in the 1980s, had extended to many more countries, and that yet others, for example Poland, were making active plans to extend the teaching of English into primary schools. The situation is, therefore, that the teaching of English to Young Learners is very much with us. It works very positively under the conditions of learning that prevail in many places, but is currently more problematical in others. The aim of this volume is, therefore, to look more closely at research that is addressing issues that can have practical application under different conditions of learning.

Different categories of Young Learners

English for Young Learners (EYL) is a convenient blanket term often used to cover English Language teaching and learning to children in a wide variety of situations. The unifying characteristic is that the English being learned is not the native or predominant home-language of the learners. The focus in this volume is on children learning in an instructional, school, situation rather than through the rarer case of only 'natural contact', but different categories of instructional situation need to be as carefully differentiated as those for English teaching in other age groups.

EFL

English as a Foreign Language (EFL) is usually taken to mean the learning and teaching of the language in situations where the use of English outside the instructional situation is not institutionalised in society – where it has no official place as the language of legislation or as the medium for some types of state-supported education. It is true to say, however, that within this definition there exist many degrees of 'foreign-ness' or 'availability', and that in many supposedly EFL countries English can actually have a very high profile.

In countries like Holland, Denmark or Israel, English is used in such a widespread way, and is to be found so readily in the local media that Young Learners can have quite an extensive contact with it day to day. In cases like this, school learning and natural exposure can be seen to interact positively in the language development of most Young Learners. In other countries English enjoys popularity and high prestige, and with the spread of satellite TV and other global media can be said to be becoming more and more 'available', but it cannot be said yet to be integrated into common daily use, or widely spoken by older generations. For Young Learners this type of EFL situation can be represented by countries such as Greece, Italy, Japan, Korea and Hungary. The common factor is that active official provision is being made for young children to learn English in the state school system. In many EFL countries there is a parallel, perhaps consequent, flourishing of classes for children in the private language school sector.

ESL

English as a Second Language (ESL) is the term used in countries in which English is officially acknowledged to have an important role alongside the local language(s) for the official business of the state and as the medium for at least some sectors of the educational system. India and Pakistan are often seen as the emblems of this role for English. However, again the wide differences from situation to situation must be recognised.

In India and Pakistan, it is perhaps true to say that English is widely used and widely taught, but there are differences in the use that different sectors of society make of it. In the case of YL, there is a broad spectrum of school types, which includes the socially elite, private English medium primary and pre-primary schools as well as state primary schools in many regions where English has no current status. In Sri Lanka, English is regarded as a second language but for many children, especially in rural areas, there is such a lack of day-to-day use of the language outside the school that the situation has more in common with an EFL one.

A similar situation exists in recently independent Namibia, where English is favoured as a second language over Afrikaans as a matter of policy and where secondary school leavers are aiming for Cambridge International General Certificate of Secondary Education (IGCSE) exam passes in English. However, English is not yet established enough in the day-to-day business of living in many areas of the country for the teachers and learners to be able to call upon its availability in the environment as a resource in the same way as can the 'EFL' teachers and learners in Israel or Holland.

EAL

In countries like Britain, Australia and the United States, English as an Additional Language (EAL) rather than ESL is the currently favoured term for the objectives for English learning that are important for the many children whose predominant home language is not English, but who find themselves in situations where English is the medium for education and for transactions and interactions in society at large. There is increasing sensitivity in these societies to issues of respect for, and maintenance of, the home language, while equipping learners to function effectively in English in the domains that concern their general welfare, social happiness and advancement in education or a profession.

Children in this type of situation will, of course, be exposed to a lot of English outside school, but it is also true to say that, for these Young Learners, English is often addressed as a particular issue within the school and given special attention for part of the school day or school week. The aim is to support children in learning the types of English needed for school work, as well as for social and practical purposes in and out of school.

A huge issue is how far lessons from one area of English Learning can validly be applied to others. For a useful overview of how EFL/ESL/EAL conditions can blend into one another see Brewster (1991).

The need for research and reflection

In a 1992 survey article of Young Learner teaching, in the journal *Language Teaching* (Rixon, 1992), I lamented the fact that there was so little recent published research available to temper or at least scrutinise some of the public 'myths' about EYL, such as 'the younger the better', or to add the weight of rigorous study to some of the areas of common classroom practice, such as story-telling, or the use of rhythmic utterances, which teachers and trainers 'felt in their bones' to be well-founded. There were also, in 1992, some conspicuously uncovered areas, such as approaches to assessing YL achievements, that needed more investigation, but had not yet been fully faced. The technicalities of appropriate syllabus content for YL and the choice of principles on which to organise lesson materials (topic-based? structural progression? functions? activity-based?) were an issue in 1992, and, I feel, are still an issue today. Beyond that, we should never forget the teacher-development issues that revolve around how teachers can be empowered to choose one type of approach over another.

Research areas covered

This volume is centred mainly around research, but research that can inform classroom practice.

Topics cover major areas of interest but relatively little previous research, such as the value of story-telling, and the role of authentic children's picture and story books (Kolsawalla and Kuhiwczak, chapters 2 and 4, respectively). There has also been very little earlier published research about Younger

Learners in areas that have been well covered for older students, such as strategy use (see Pinter chapter 1). In the early years of the YL 'boom' many newly introduced projects for the introduction of English to Young Learners were still at the experimental stage and had not 'come of age' in the sense that there had, as yet, been little or no requirement to integrate them with practices that were mandatory in other curriculum subjects. The requirement for YL to be assessed is one of the major signs that English is an established part of the primary school curriculum. In many countries, issues about assessment are having to be addressed quite urgently both for periodic in-school assessment purposes, and for purposes of preparing reports on children's achievements in English, along with other subjects, that could well affect their placement in a new school. Many of the countries in which YL are taught English have also quite recently instituted evaluation projects that involve assessment of pupils' achievements as one part of a study that is designed to 'show the benefit' – to help to modify teaching practices at the Primary level and to help with planning how the transition from one level of schooling to another might best be confronted. Chapter 7 on assessment, by Rea-Dickins and Rixon, attempts to raise issues in both these areas where assessment can have a role.

Chapters 3 and 5 (Nesi and Rixon) are about different aspects of materials' design. Rixon's study concerns the extremely diverse vocabulary content of published materials and how this might affect what teachers can do, guided by the book, or independent of it, if the book is essentially their 'syllabus', whereas Nesi looks at the quantity and type of information that is most useful to Young Learners in a dictionary specially designed for them. Nikolov presents an interesting account of Young Learners' code-switching in English lessons, through data captured by unobtrusive recording of normal classroom activities.

A gamut of research procedures is presented in this volume, from the wide-ranging, such as surveys based on questionnaires (chapter 7) or large-scale testing (Nesi, chapter 3), to more delicate and detailed procedures, such as ways of approaching detailed elicitation of children's recall of language items (chapter 2) or of designing tasks and analysis procedures to capture children's communication strategies.

Where a special statistical procedure has been used to analyse data, there are notes on its use in a special section at the end of the volume (pages 102–103).

A major policy decision and 'slant' in the whole volume has been towards studies that, at least at some stage, investigated the learners directly, or asked the learners what they felt or thought. We feel that this is highly important. In a world where adults tend to make the decisions that EYL teaching is a 'good thing' for a number of not always carefully analysed reasons it is refreshing and illuminating, as well as ethically desirable, to try to give the children a voice, even if it is only about their reactions to what has already been decided for them, and not about whether they would have voted for it themselves in that particular form.

Applicability of the research to other situations

In any research project, there is always the tension between capturing accurately what is special and particular about a situation, in terms of the conditions of learning and teaching and the values that are current, and trying to generalise to more universally applicable findings that might illuminate what children in general 'can/will do' and how they feel, regardless of their home culture and language, the teaching culture in which they are largely 'pawns in the game', or the wider society in which they are placed, with all its values and opinions. The researches presented in this volume are often small-scale and localised, and thus the writers do not claim that they can be universally applicable, but, on the other hand, some of the results and insights may be very recognisable to teachers from other situations, who might thus be inspired to replicate the research or undertake a similar study to verify or challenge the results.

1 Investigations into Task-related Strategy Use with Young Learners of English

Annamaria Pinter
*Centre for English Language Teacher Education,
University of Warwick*

This article will examine how four communication tasks prompt or encourage children to use certain strategies. It compares which tasks children find easier to carry out successfully, and describes the strategies used, as well as some of the difficulties which may be inherent in the actual task itself.

Background to the study

According to Nunan (1989:11), who surveyed the literature to find an overall definition for what a communication task in language teaching is, the following is a good summary of what various researchers and teachers accept as a definition: 'the task is a piece of meaning-focused work involving learners in comprehending, producing and/or interacting in the target language'. He also points out that tasks are analysed and categorised according to their goals, input data, activities, settings and roles. Willis (1996) contributes to this definition by saying that task activities are ones where the target language is used by the learner for communicative purposes (goals) in order to achieve an outcome.

Task-based research has taken two main directions. One is concerned with investigations into second language acquisition. The main purpose of this line of research is to find out which tasks under what circumstances will facilitate the negotiation of meaning and thus, through modified input, the internalisation of new language (interaction theory of language acquisition). These research projects link task-based interaction with communication-processing theories and are interested in issues such as change-of-task performance features upon repeated exposure to the task.

The other line of research is related to task structures and performance outcomes with the primary aim of improving instructional materials and practices. The question they ask is to do with how resources can be manipulated to produce task-related, communicatively effective messages. Yule and Powers (1994:81) argue strongly for the importance of this line of research: 'Specifically, there has been virtually no interest in determining whether, as a result of taking part in particular types of interaction, the NNS [non-native speaker] appears to develop more effective communicative skills or not'.

My paper follows the second approach, since it is trying to find out how the actual structures of the task determine the way children manage the interaction and how effective their communication skills prove to be.

The tasks investigate spoken performance, which is the type described by Brown and Yule (1983) as the transactional function of language, i.e. message-oriented interaction. The tasks are all referential communication tasks as defined by Yule (1997:1):

> ... the term given to communicative acts, generally spoken, in which some kind of information is exchanged between two speakers. This information exchange is typically dependent on successful acts of reference, whereby entities (human or non-human) are identified (by naming or describing), are located or moved relative to other entities (by giving instructions or directions), or are followed through sequences of locations and events (by recounting an incident or a narrative).

The tasks introduced in this article are also characterised by the features Brown *et al.* (1984) define as static tasks. This means that the transfer of the message only requires the description and manipulation of static objects. No dynamic elements are introduced to move these objects in space or time. Similarly, abstract features are avoided thus ensuring there is no need to discuss hypothetical relationships. All four tasks of mine belong to the category of static referential communication tasks.

The tasks
- Picture recognition – speaker A describes his pictures while speaker B must identify the pictures among his distractors.
- Spot the difference – speakers A and B work together on discovering differences between their sets of pictures.
- Describe and draw – speaker A describes his picture to B who has to draw it.
- Picture reconstruction – speakers A and B work together to complete their pictures from the information obtained from each other.

The data
The spoken output of the four tasks was recorded with Hungarian children who are learning English as a foreign language in the primary school. The total corpus is about 13,000 words, gathered from ten pairs of children recorded on all four tasks. The children are all ten years old and have been learning English for three years. They were selected as high achievers in English for this experiment and they were all very eager and enthusiastic about the tasks. I was present in all the recordings as an interlocutor, and also as a source of help and information for them.

Analysis of tasks
The four tasks are similar in that they require decentering on the speaker's part, i.e. the recognition that others typically do not already know/see what the self obviously does (Yule, 1997). Referential communication does not develop automatically, even in the mother tongue, so one question this paper asks is to what

extent some tasks will prompt children to use more effective strategies for transferring information.

Even though the tasks described seem relatively similar (they all use visual input and the same vocabulary), they have different internal structural features and therefore put varying demands on learners. First of all, two of the tasks (1 and 3) are one-way tasks: speaker A holds the information that will have to be communicated, and so the flow of information is one-way. The other two tasks (2 and 4) are two-way: it is the joint responsibility of both speakers to initiate the interaction since they both possess information that needs to be communicated to the other person.

The interaction in all tasks is obligatory rather than optional (Pica et al., 1993). In all tasks it was emphasised to both children that they could speak, ask questions or clarify statements when they liked. The participants in all four cases are working towards a convergent rather than a divergent goal (Duff, 1986).

Continuing with in-built structural factors, 'picture reconstruction' and 'describe and draw' are both 'low control' tasks (though not to the same extent) since it is up to the children to decide how much detail they want to go into when describing their pictures and the items they have to draw. The task structure does not inherently guarantee that certain language will be produced. On the other hand, the other two tasks – 'picture recognition', and 'spot the difference' – are more controlled in the sense that the specific detail children have to identify in the pictures is more easily isolated, and the performance is more predictable because specific linguistic hurdles have to be overcome to carry out the task successfully.

Time pressure also differs in each task. The 'describe and draw' task represents the lowest time pressure since there is plenty of time for the speaker to think while the partner is drawing. In the case of 'picture reconstruction' there is also time to think and look at the picture before having to speak. When roles are not specified in two-way tasks as 'information provider' and 'receiver', there is less pressure on the particular individual to have to speak. Time pressure is greatest with the 'picture recognition' task, since the speaker is forced to provide as much information as quickly as possible to the other person so he can select a picture among the distractors.

Other task variables

BACKGROUND: All children come from the same educational background, and have experienced the same style of learning/teaching. The proficiency level of the children as well as their age is the same.

SETTING: All children were recorded on school premises out of the classroom with a friend of their own choice as a partner. Gender differences were not possible to control, although it is recognised that gender may play a role as to how the interactions proceed. The children all heard the same instructions and introduction and they all perceived me as an outsider who has no authority over them at school. They were all extremely enthusiastic to help and seemed not to be at all disturbed by the tape-recorder.

TASKS: All four tasks were administered to each pair of children in a random order. The tasks were not familiar to them except for the 'describe and draw' task which some of them mentioned they had come across before.

Results

Although the outcomes of the analysis of the interaction are interpretable at various levels, this paper will only concentrate on examining the task-related strategies, those which, due to the inherent structure, help or hinder the children in managing the task more or less successfully. Task performance is considered successful when the intended transfer of information has been achieved. Grammatical accuracy or efficiency in terms of time are not understood here as contributing towards success.

Whatever the children say is in small print. The words in *italics* are my comments. It is also indicated when children use L1 (native language) rather than L2 (English) to communicate.

Picture recognition

The object of the task is for speaker A to describe a picture so that B can choose the same one among his distractors. If we examine the steps taken by children in managing this task, the usual pattern that emerges is this: speaker A will give a description of one picture and then B will make a decision, in an ideal case, by eliminating all the distractors in front of him, as to which picture is being described. However, on closer examination this general pattern gets more complicated.

After A has described a picture, B may choose a picture immediately and get it right as a result of an adequate description or possibly by pure luck. If B gets it wrong, speaker A will acknowledge the mistake and give negative feedback, or B asks clarifying questions until a decision can be made safely about which picture is being described. Alternatively, speaker A may take the initiative and provide extra information probably based on the distractors that he or she can also see. After the questions or extra information, speaker B can again attempt to make a decision which will either be right or wrong, as we have seen above. Each interaction may be described as a sequence of several steps.

Picture 1 and picture 3 (see Figure 1, page 5) proved to be easier than the other two, since all the interactions finished with a carefully eliminated choice, whereas in the case of picture 2 and 4, six interactions altogether finished with an 'accidentally' right choice.

There are several strategies here which can be considered successful and desirable. The first and most obvious one is speaker A oriented. If the description is adequate and precise, and if the message is conveyed clearly, B can immediately make an informed decision, for example:

EXTRACT 1 (PICTURE 1)
>A: I have got a red house. And two people. The house is big. The girl have purple dress.
>B: OK.
>*(B makes a correct choice.)*

Picture 1 plus one distractor with a tree and children on the other side of the house; the other distractor with different-looking children.

Picture 2 plus one distractor with a smaller piece of cheese; the other distractor with a different-looking monster.

Picture 3 plus one distractor with one fish of a different colour; the other distractor with two extra snakes.

Picture 4 plus one distractor with a different-coloured clock and flag on the castle; the other distractor with the ball behind the monkey.

Figure 1 Picture recognition. One child (A) has one of the above pictures to describe and the other child (B) has the same, plus two distractors to chose from. (All pictures in colour)

Equally successful is another method whereby speaker B takes a more active role and asks clarifying questions, and thus systematically eliminates the distractors one by one:

EXTRACT 2 (PICTURE 1)
    A: There are one house, one house in this picture.
    B: OK.
    A: There are one girl in the picture, there are one boy in the picture, the house, it is pink.
    B: Windows?
    A: I can see seven windows in the picture.
    B: Can you see a cap on the girl's head?
    A: Yes.
    (B makes the correct choice.)

All interactions finish with B choosing the right picture either as a result of careful elimination or by pure luck. Speaker A can see all the distractors of B, and therefore by looking and comparing the visuals, the discrepancies can eventually be eliminated, so speaker A will never accept any other solution than the correct one. In this respect, this task offers a lot more support visually than 'spot the difference'. Letting speaker A see B's pictures helps children avoid one of the traps they would fall into if the task was 'purely one-way', i.e. if A could not see B's pictures. While the information is still held by one person, the distractors are seen by both partners and thus the task is made friendlier and suits the children better.

This factor has a clear influence on the success rate of this task (which is measured here by how many pairs out of the total managed to complete the task successfully, i.e. transfer information and choose the right picture). This task is certainly the winner among the four tasks, with only six instances of problematic solutions out of a total of 36 interactions analysed (due to a technical problem only nine pairs were recorded, which means nine times four pictures altogether).

One would think that the chances for problematic solutions are very slight, but in fact this is not the case:

EXTRACT 3 (PICTURE 4)
    A: Ball, monkey.
    B: This?
    A: No, because the castle clock red.
    B: The monkey in front of the ball?
    A: Yes.
    B: This one.
    A: Yes.
    (B chooses the right picture but there is no correspondence between what is said and what is seen.)

In this case the problem is that these girls were not confident about the prepositions. First, speaker B attempted to ask a question which involved the use of a preposition 'in front of' and speaker A, probably being unsure about what the preposition meant but at the same time happy that the other person provided the word, just took it for granted that 'in front of' was the right preposition to describe the original picture. As a result, B made a correct choice by selecting the same picture, but in fact the preposition in the picture should have been 'behind' rather than 'in front of'. Speaker A accepted it by probably glancing at the two visuals and recognising they were the same. They both used and understood 'in front of' as something else, probably meaning 'behind' and the lucky match of the same visuals only reinforced their interpretations. There is no way one can avoid such traps in these tasks, since it is always possible that two speakers will agree on something that is actually wrong, just because one follows the other, and neither of them is sure about the language used. As far as possible, this task minimises the chances of this occurring (which is evident from the data since it occurred only once) by providing the visuals. The problem is more serious as soon as this support is taken away (see: 'Spot the difference' task).

All the other instances occurred because the questioning on the part of the listener (speaker B) was not consistent and methodical, i.e. did not cover all the possible points of difference in the distractors one by one, and, when the choice was made, it was made by guessing. Sometimes, B did not even ask a clarifying question but made a choice immediately and by luck got the right picture. This on the surface looks like a very efficient way of dealing with the task. In fact the opposite is true, these children did not exhibit any systematic approach to eliminating the options. They made a wild guess which worked for them and this may even have encouraged them to use guessing as a strategy to deal with the task.

Spot the difference
The object of the game is to identify the difference between two similar pictures without seeing each other's visuals, so that each interaction finishes as soon as the real or the perceived discrepancy has been found. Since the roles are not fixed here, the proportion of the output by the two children is different from the previous task. In this case speaker A does not necessarily initiate the interaction and the information to be communicated is a shared responsibility, so the patterns of interaction will change. The kind of question/statement that can be asked/stated includes a sequence and various combinations of the following:
- Have you got X?
- Have you got A X? (adjective + noun)
- Is your X somewhere? (location)
- Is your X a certain colour? (colour)
- Has your X got other descriptive features? (e.g. somebody wearing something)
- How many of X have you got? (number)

The success rate is lower than with the previous task. Some pictures (see Figure 2, page 8) proved to be more demanding, leading to perceived differences or even a lack of solution. The set of pictures with a difference in the location of

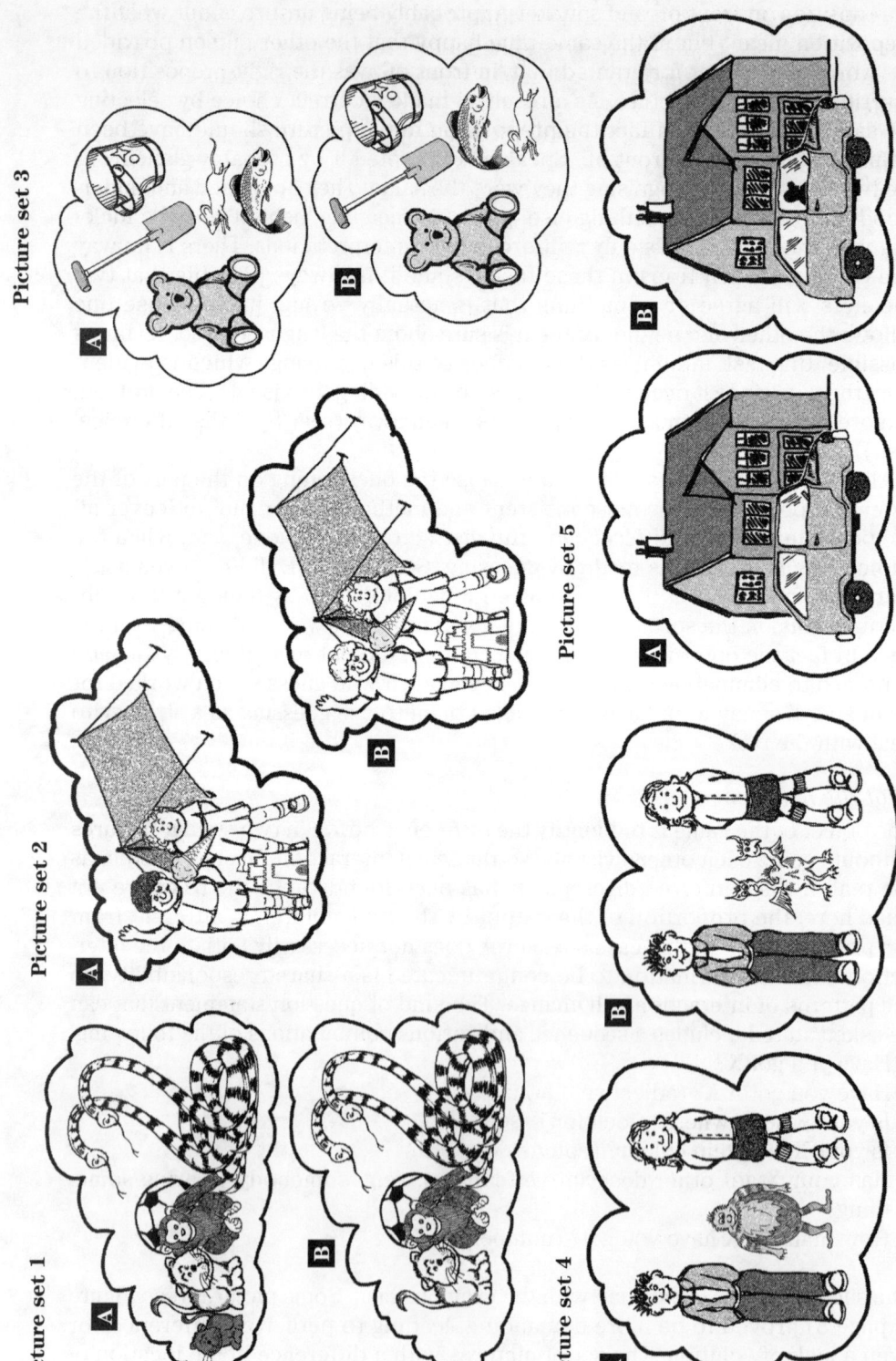

Figure 2 Spot the difference

the object (set 3) clearly caused most difficulty with the children: only one pair managed to work out the difference without any prompting or help. Descriptive feature differences seemed to work much better, and missing items caused no problem either.

There was a difference between the two missing-item pictures. In the case of picture set 1, the missing item was a little black cat while both children had a big white cat in their picture. So, one would expect that with attentive listening both partners have a chance to pick up on the difference. If one of them says, 'I have got two cats' even without further details, this statement should be enough to signal the difference to the other person. Or, alternatively, the other speaker by saying, 'I have got a cat' without any other details, again should be able to signal the difference. In the case of some very attentive listeners this is what happens, but the majority ignored these initial signs of difference.

EXTRACT 4 (PICTURE SET 1)
    A: A black small cat, no, a black white cat.
    B: Big white cat.
    A: Yes ... The monkey colour is brown.
(Although 'a small black cat' and 'a big white cat' were linguistically distinguished and contrasted, no acknowledgement of the difference was stated, the difference was ignored and the interaction continued with other objects.)

It is postulated that these children do not actually react to the difference because they are waiting for the interlocutor to acknowledge it. In other words, they think it is the job of the interlocutor to decide when the exercise is finished.

The other set of pictures which had a missing item is set 5. Here one child had a driver in the car and the other did not. This difference is slightly more difficult for them to spot, since if you have an empty car, you are very unlikely to point out this emptiness, whereas if you have a driver, you will probably mention him as an important feature. This means that one speaker is more likely to mention the difference than the other, so the chances that the point gets discussed are less than in the previous missing-item set.

As far as the strategies are concerned, this task seems to be problematic in that no matter how systematic or attentive you are, it still depends on luck whether you will find the difference quickly or not. Sometimes children just stumble across the difference without having to put any effort into it at all. But, it also happens that they use all the essentially good strategies of systematically going through the details and only find the difference after a long struggle. Compare extracts 5 and 6 for picture set 4:

EXTRACT 5 (PICTURE SET 4)
    A: I can see a monster in the picture, a monster.
    B: Yes.
    A: The monster two head.
    B: No, I haven't.

(By pure luck these children start discussing the monster rather than the other two figures in the picture.)

Contrast this with the following dialogue:

EXTRACT 6 (PICTURE SET 4)
    A: In this picture is one mum and one father, one mother and one father and one dragon. The dragon is green.
    B: The mum, the mother is, has got blue pullover.
    A: Yes, the mother's shoes are white, the mother knee is white. The mother's skirt is black.
    B: Yes, and the father's trousers are purple.
    A: Yes.
    B: The father's pullover is green.
    A: Yes.
    B: The mother's hair is orange.
    A: Yes.
    B: The father's hair is black.
    A: Yes.
    B: The dragon, between the father and the mother.
    A: Yes.

At this point they want to give up and say they have not got any differences in their pictures. They are prompted to continue, but not prompted about the nature of the difference they are looking for.

    B: The father has got white shoes.
    A: What?
    B: Shoes. The father has got black and white shoes.
    A: Yes.
    B: The dragon has got two head.
    A: No, no, the dragon has one head.
    (This is where the difference is finally found.)

One important strategy – being attentive to what the other person says – is crucial here (as always) and would sometimes help children cut down on the number of question/response routines they have to go through. Attentiveness was important in the previous task as well, but, as we saw, possible lack of attentiveness was compensated for by having the visuals accessible to speaker A for comparison. Most children find it difficult to pay attention to the other person's description, especially if it is fairly long and contains information about more than one object. Some are aware that they are unable to listen, concentrate, take in all the information, and instead use a strategy of asking the partner to repeat the information, either directly or indirectly. Where some children fail is that they concentrate rather on what *they* want to say next and just ignore the other speaker completely. This can of course be a simultaneous problem for both speakers and can result in finding a difference, linguistically pointing it out, but not acknowledging it in any way by saying 'finished' or 'we have found it' or 'this is the difference'. Instead, they carry on asking routine questions desperately (as in extract 4 above).

Due to the overwhelming effect of pure luck, it is very hard to identify strategies of management other than above. Perhaps, if the task was such that one had to find several differences within the same picture, it would pay off to be more systematic and consistent with the questions and descriptions. So, all in all, it is partly the structure of the task that inherently pushes the emphasis towards luck rather than strategies.

As far as the breakdown of the kind of questions the children ask is concerned, not surprisingly, most questions are about colours (141 altogether out of the total of 425 questions). This number is even more significant if we add those that ask about other descriptive features, a lot of which contain reference to colours as well, e.g. the 'boy's got a white shirt on'. If we add the two categories together, the number of these questions represents more than 50 per cent of all questions asked in total (229 out of 425 questions).

It is noticeable how the kinds of objects illustrated in individual pictures can influence the proportion of question types asked, even though it seems that colours and descriptive features are overwhelmingly dominant and also easiest for these children to use. The high proportion of colour questions is also a result of a strategy which children use in order to play safe. Once they have found a question type that they are confident with, they try to use it as much as possible to exploit all the opportunities for colours, for example, in their picture. This obvious overuse of colour questions can also be explained by a well-described phenomenon in the literature called utilisation deficiency (for a review of utilisation deficiencies see Miller and Seier, 1994). What this means is that children under various task circumstances tend to keep using a strategy despite the obvious lack of benefit from it.

Describe and draw

The goal of the task was to describe a picture (see Figure 3, page 12) to the other person so that he or she can reproduce the drawings as accurately as possible. The typical pattern to be followed is this: children name the objects they can see, give descriptive features if they can, at least colours, if nothing else. It was up to the children to choose which picture they wanted to describe and it was also up to them to decide in what detail they wished to describe them. Although they did not have a lot of time to choose the pictures, the one with the monsters was the most popular for several reasons. One is that in the case of the monsters, prepositions are not so relevant or important, which is obviously an area that a lot of children struggle with. Also, in terms of vocabulary, there are several descriptive features to talk about (all within the topic of 'parts of the body' and, if you know one item, you usually know all the others). All the other pictures are a bit more cluttered, the positions of the various objects being important (e.g. picture 1, with a house, some tents and trees, leaves quite a lot of scope for the person who is drawing to arrange them in various ways in the physical space available). Another reason why the one with the monsters got selected over the others is that it is a well known and popular topic from children's course books and so could have seemed more familiar.

Figure 3 Describe and draw

On closer observation a contradiction between producing a picture as close to the original as possible and at the same time as quickly as possible is revealed. This tension may have affected children in different ways. They were all told that the goal of the task was to produce identical pictures (and indeed this has to the objective criterion for success), but they were also told that they had to do this as quickly as possible for the activity to proceed at a reasonable speed. There is no way of knowing which priority children considered more important. Although this did not cause any overt problems, it adds to the degree of open-endedness in the task.

Because of the open-endedness of this task it is difficult to analyse the language and make numerical comparisons, but it is certainly possible to look at some of the strategies children use to deal with the task. First of all they choose a picture with which they foresee least problems in terms of vocabulary, familiarity, etc. Once they have found a pattern of describing features or questions they are comfortable with, it seems that they stretch the use of those well-known expressions/patterns to exploit the knowledge they have.

EXTRACT 7 (PICTURE 3)
    A: The monster is green. The monster is big mouth. The monster is red teeth. The monster is green, three grey eyes.
    B: Is that all right ? (L1)
    A: The monster is big blue, big blue and big nose. The monster is short legs. The monster is short, short hands. The monster is big tongue. The monster is ...

The monster picture is evidently excellent in this respect because once one monster has been successfully described and drawn, the other two will follow the same routine. Children can, therefore, start to relax, enjoy what they are doing, show wit and humour. Some children even ask questions which have little to do with the picture in context, I suspect, just to exhibit their knowledge and impress the interlocutor. For example, one girl asks the question: 'Has the monkey got a banana?' In the context where different animals are described to her, and none of those animals have got anything at all, it seems that the only reason to ask the question is to show, 'Look I know a word which I can show off with'. And, after all, why not? Some children get so relaxed that they start to socialise and chat to each other in their native tongue (L1). Because of the openness of the task, children are given the opportunity to relax a bit.

For less confident children there are no in-built hurdles in the task that one *must* get through. If it was necessary, they could do the task at a minimal level, which basically means listing the objects in the picture and ignoring locations where possible. And some of them indeed chose to follow this minimalist approach. It is possible that these children considered the timing of the activity more important than the artistic details of how similar the drawings turned out.

EXTRACT 8 (PICTURE 4)
    A: Two cats. One cat is ...
    B: Wait, wait. (L1)
    A: ... white and one is black.
    B: Wait a minute. (L1)

Figure 4 Picture reconstruction

A: One fish, the fish is orange and a black eyes, eye, black, and one monkey, monkey eyes is blue and black, blue, black, blue and black and the red mouth and the monkey is brown.

Picture reconstruction

The object of the task is to complete the picture (see Figure 4, page 14), some features of which they both share, for the sake of being able to establish reference points. Whatever speaker A is missing, speaker B has got, and *vice versa*. Also, where something is missing, a little cloud indicates to the child that a question must be asked and an object must be recovered.

The interaction pattern to complete the task successfully would look like this:
- Ask about/identify one or more reference points.
- Make sure you get a positive response when you are establishing common reference points.
- Use the reference points and ask about your missing item.
- Confirm and clarify the response before drawing it in the slot.
- If the other person can't follow you, go back to a known reference point and try again with something else.
- Signal if you want to jump from one picture to another.

There were no pairs which followed this pattern. Some children did not try to establish common reference points at all, but just started asking about their missing items in random order. It was very common for them to jump all over the picture, back and forth, sometimes with, sometimes without, signalling. On average a pair jumped from one part of the picture to the other three to four times during the interaction. As soon as they found out what the missing item was, they automatically drew it into the next slot, paying no attention to location.

The biggest challenge they had to deal with was located in the second part of picture set 2, which had three boys in it. One was a safe reference point for everybody (the one with a spade and bucket). The two other boys were missing, one for each speaker. Seven out of the ten interactions did not manage to work out correctly which boy was where. This task resulted in the most difficult problem to solve due to a lack of ability to deal with multiple referencing. All in all, this was the task where most L1 was spoken, most instructions were given, and children used most clarifications, both in L1 and L2. Consider this example:

EXTRACT 9 (PICTURE SET 2)
    A: I have got two green snakes. A little boy and a big ice-cream.
    (These features are far away from each other and the location is not signalled at all.)
    Have you got them? (Question asked in L1.)
    (There is no response to this question but A decides to go on.)
    The ice-cream colour is yellow.
    B: The ice-cream itself? (Question asked in L1.)
    A: Yes, the whole ice-cream. (Response in L1.)

(Here A decides to move on to the boy who has got the ice-cream and says:)
The boy's hair is black. His T-shirt is red. His T-shirt is red.
B: Talk about the one with the tents on. (In L1.)
(Instruction given in L1 because the speaker is not sure what is going on.)
A: That is what I am talking about. (Response in L1 again.)
B: Say it again then. (In L1.)
A: Big yellow ice-cream.

Summary of findings

There are three immediately observable strategies children use in all four tasks. A particular strategy may be more strongly associated with one or two particular tasks, but overall, all these strategies are detectable all over the corpus.

- The first one is *'using L1'* in order to double check words or expressions not available in L2, and to engage in task-related discourse to establish common grounds about the task before carrying it out. Task 4 in particular prompted a lot of use of the L1, but the tendency is the same everywhere.
- The second strategy is *'appealing for assistance'*. This is a specific case of using L1, exclusively targeted towards the adult present. It means signalling implicitly or explicitly that you do not see a way out of the task and want some help. Very often, however, children approach the adult with queries that would not be absolutely essential for carrying out the task. They just make use of the constant availability of the adult to satisfy their curiosity.
- The third strategy is *'building patterns'* whereby children repeat what they are comfortable with over and over again. They play safe and try to exploit a given phrase as much as possible. This is especially noticeable during tasks 3 and 4.

In addition to the above, the data also throws up other strategies which can be analysed as the by-product or even the limitation of one particular task. Task 1 (picture recognition), by providing mutually shared visual support, builds a great deal of safety into the interaction, but even this visual support cannot guarantee that misunderstandings will be avoided. Although, it must be said, when children jump to conclusions and make hasty decisions, the visuals very often help them towards successful task completion, it is often the visual prompt rather than any linguistic negotiation that pushes children towards the solution.

In the case of task 2 (spot the difference), the fact that there is only one difference in each picture caused a lot of trouble. This is definitely a structural flaw which ultimately encourages children to guess rather than eliminate the features one by one. More misunderstandings than on the previous task occurred, and a considerable number of interactions came to an end without finding the real differences.

Task 3 (describe and draw) seems to highlight the problem of open-ended tasks very clearly. There is an inherent tension between two competing priorities: the quality of the artistic reproduction and a fast, efficient progression with the task. This task also encourages minimal contributions from children who, for a particular reason, do not wish to take risks at all.

Task 4 (picture reconstruction) presented most problems to the children and resulted in a great deal of confusion and non-understanding. This may have been due to the referential pressure built into the task, or the artificiality of the whole activity, or the fact that the task was not fully understood by the children. L1 data could helpfully complement the results here. Whatever their difficulty, children showed very little consistency in dealing with this task.

The findings regarding children's strategies on these tasks and the kind of problems particular tasks hide are tentative for a number of reasons. First of all the data should be further analysed from various other perspectives, such as the communication strategies used, the quality of the meaning negotiations, and other features of the spoken output. This would ensure that our understanding of what exactly happens on these tasks would be considerably widened. Secondly, it would be necessary to compare/contrast this data with baseline data yielded in L1 on the same tasks to clearly isolate the effects of a foreign-language medium. Finally, the results are to be handled with caution because the interactions were carried out under very special circumstances, out of the classroom, with an adult present all the time. My findings therefore cannot *directly* inform classroom practice since my concern is with the tasks as 'raw materials'. However, before these tasks or similar ones are to be used in the classroom, the first step for the teacher must be to analyse the internal structure of the tasks and discover hidden problems inherent in them. I believe that the above analysis of what exactly happened when the four tasks were administered to children does exactly that.

2 Teaching Vocabulary Through Rhythmic Refrains in Stories

Havovi Kolsawalla
British Council, Bombay

It has often been hypothesised that rhythmic utterances aid memorisation of their form and content. One of the most popular formats for stories to be told to children is that in which a rhythmic section (refrain) is repeated many times, and this has often been observed to result in spontaneous 'joining in' by the young audience. Teachers of Young Learners of a language often feel from experience that this exposure to rhythmic utterances benefits retention of words in memory, but few systematic studies have been made of this phenomenon.

A small-scale investigation was therefore designed to investigate whether young children exposed to such a story-telling experience would retain stressed 'key' items from the story better when they were in the context of a rhythmic refrain than when they appeared in the narrative body of the story. Two matched groups of 5–6 year-old pupils in a Coventry school, from backgrounds in which English was not the main home language, were told two different versions of the same story in which key vocabulary items were differently distributed between the 'rhythmic refrain' and the 'prose narrative'. The children's memory for these items was checked immediately after the story-telling experience and results were clear-cut in favour of retention in the short term of items found in the rhythmic refrain.

In support of story-telling

Both the range and quality of exposure that a language learner receives within the teaching and learning situation will affect his/her ability to use the language (Daughty and Thorton, 1972). 'Multiple presentations ... as well ... as multiple opportunities for the learner to practise ...' (Spolsky, 1989:199) are considered an important condition in second language development. So, adequate exposure to the target language is of prime importance in language learning, but the greatest problem that faces an ESL or EFL teacher is how to combine adequate quality of exposure, that is, language use in meaningful contexts, with adequate quantity of exposure. In cases where exposure to the second language is limited mainly or only to what is provided in the school environment, finding solutions to this problem becomes especially crucial.

To Young Learners, few contexts are more meaningful than a story. 'When you tell a story you are speaking their language' (Ferrell and Nessel, 1982). That children's interest in stories is strong and powerful is evident from the quality of attention they engage. It is therefore highly opportune if teachers recognise the value of story-telling as a pedagogical tool rather than considering it to be mere 'play' (Barton, 1986; Stewig, 1978; Garvie, 1989; Rixon, 1991). A story, with its elements of novelty, humour, conflict and surprise, heightens the arousal level (Berylene, 1960) and this in turn creates its own motivation to attend to the situation and learn from the context. The context then is at once 'purposive and pleasurable' (Travers, 1988). It at once stimulates interest and provides the foundation for language development. Moreover, since story-telling is not traditionally associated with 'learning', the 'affective filter' level is low (Krashen, 1981) and this also is an advantage in the learning process as the learner absorbs and assimilates more than in a formal teaching/learning situation.

Story-telling is very closely linked with teaching through the use of themes or topics. Thematic or topic-based teaching has been particularly advocated in recent years as an effective condition in the teaching/learning process in general and even more so for Young Learners of a language (Holderness, 1991). An interesting theme provides motivation for learning and engages the learners' attention. It also provides the opportunity to create networks of words either related in meaning or belonging to the same genre of things, or words connected to a particular concept or theme. A theme can be expounded through the use of visual aids or general discussion, but a story has added power in that it not only generates interest but it is also structured. It is a 'cohesive device' (Garvie, 1989) which contains in it an exposition of thought and language.

By listening to stories children are introduced to a number of words in context. Very often repeated use of words in the same context, or in varying contexts, helps them to infer the meanings of words and gradually assimilate them into their growing lexicon (Barton, 1986).

As mentioned earlier (Spolsky, 1989), multiple presentation of linguistic material ranks high in the conditions for successful language learning, but children do not generally like to hear the same material repeated to them without good reason. However, the fact that many good stories contain just such motivated repetition within themselves, and also that children love to listen to a story over and over again, day after day or week after week, provides them with repeated association with words and therefore helps them to internalise their meaning and use (Trelease, 1982).

Stories which have rhythmic refrains repeated at regular intervals have an added advantage. It has often been observed that on hearing the refrain children learn to anticipate it and then join in with the words they remember. 'Patterns ring in their ears and seduce them to join in' (Barton and Booth, 1990).

In story-telling there is no pressure on individual children to produce language until they are ready to do so and join in with the narration of their own accord. It is widely observed, however, that children seem very ready to 'join in' at an early stage, and the consequent choral contribution to a well-told tale becomes both a satisfying and unthreatening way for the class to participate. In this way, words and phrases that are included in the story are produced, maybe mechanically at first, but then, with repeated association as the story is heard over and over again, these words are included in the creative production of language.

The 1990s have shown a return of research interest in the value of such 'chunks', 'formulaic utterances' or 'pre-fabs' as a route to positive language-learning strategies in all learners, including children. At one level the chunk may remain unanalysed and be produced in all contexts exactly as it was internalised, but later stages of learning may involve treating it as a framework within which some lexical elements may be substituted to fit the context. Syntactic adjustments may also be applied to make the utterance fit the particular context of the discourse. Formulaic utterances thus become templates for the learners' own 'customised' utterances, and as such may be seen as highly important for a view of learning that promotes accuracy of language use alongside the fluency that the availability of such templates is widely hypothesised to support. (See Weinert, 1995 for more discussion of this important point.)

Story-telling, then, is a very 'natural approach' to second language development and provides conditions comparable to those involved in the learning of the mother tongue. It provides a 'double bill' of entertainment and learning, the former being more evident to the learner than the latter. The role of the teacher is then that of a facilitator rather than of an instructor as the learners bring with them the means and motivation for learning and are ready for the input of the target language. Story-telling, therefore, is one way of compensating for the lack of target language exposure that a learner suffers when not much of the second or foreign language is heard in the community at large.

In support of rhythm

In normal speech the information-bearing, content, words of a message contain a stressed syllable (Gimson, 1994:261). Normal English speech is often characterised as 'stress-timed', that is highly regular in its rhythmic patterning, since the time intervals between stressed syllables tend towards equal duration. This is an area of some controversy in its details for normal speech (see Roach, 1993: 120–123), but it is generally agreed that English utterances can be readily and deliberately converted into highly regular rhythmic form when fixed formulae such as proverbs, clichéd sayings and repeated phrases are involved, not to mention verse forms in nursery rhymes or limericks. The repeated refrains of many well-loved stories, (e.g. Chicken Licken's 'Oh the sky is falling and I must go and tell the King'), as well as the formulae involved, e.g. 'Once upon a time ...', 'And that was the end of the wicked witch/troll/wolf', are certainly highly regular and striking in their rhythmic patterning.

A child's fascination with rhythm is evident from a very early age. 'Among the various methods used by children in their efforts to learn their spoken language, the arrangement of words in certain patterns plays a significant role' (Chukovsky, 1971:61). As children hear adults repeating rhymes to them, they pick up words and phrases in the rhythm of the verse. At times the words that are 'repeated back' by the children may be utter gibberish, but what is strongly adhered to is the rhythm. It is this 'inner chime' that children respond to in their understanding and use of language (Comeaux, 1981).

The precise reason why rhythm is so memorable to a listener is still under discussion, but it has been pointed out by Clark and Clark (1977:288) that 'Regular articulatory patterns are easier to pronounce than irregular ones'. Also, it has been shown that disruption of rhythm has a negative effect on the immediate recall of words (Du Preez, 1974) and this may be because rhythm provides the listeners with 'a predictable structure on which to hang their linguistic processing' (Taylor, 1990). It may be extrapolated that rhythmic lines have the dual function of both liberating and arresting the attention of listener and speaker alike. Rhythm is liberating because it follows a regular pattern and attention is not diverted to detect the stressed syllables or words. By the very feature of its periodicity, rhythm gives listeners a chance to anticipate what is coming (Martin, 1972). Therefore the child is free to pick up the content words from the other words that are uttered. Thus, we find possible reasons for the fact that stories which have a rhythmical refrain are very popular with children. They satisfy their innate fascination with language and its rhythmical sounds.

The experiment

Bringing together views summarised in the above brief review of the literature and my personal experience with Young Learners, an experiment was designed to test the hypothesis that rhythmic refrains that are repeated often in a story are more memorable verbatim than other parts of the story. Narrowing down the argument for experimental purposes, it was hypothesised that content words stressed within these deliberately highly salient sections of a story would be more easily recalled than content words in other parts of the story.

The subjects

A class of students aged around five, learning English as an Additional Language in the reception class of a British primary school in Coventry was chosen. From the pre-experiment investigation it seems safe to say that English was not used in the home in any major way.

The reception class was chosen because for many of the students it was the first year of learning English in school and therefore the experiment would indicate how vocabulary can be taught and learnt at the elementary level.

Procedures

1 VISITS Preparatory visits were made to the school, to develop a rapport with the students, to interview them and gauge their responses to storytelling.

2 STRUCTURED INTERVIEWS Structured interviews with students were conducted to ascertain what language was spoken at home with parents, siblings and friends. It helped to confirm that, for these particular pupils, English was only used in school.

3 QUESTIONNAIRE The class teacher was given a questionnaire to assess the language level of each student and this helped to divide them into two matched mixed-ability groups of 12 students each.

4 PILOTING OF THE STORY-TELLING EXPERIENCE During the preparatory visits, the students were told stories by the experimenter in order to do the following:
a) acquaint the students with the experimenter's style of telling stories;
b) gain an insight into the reactions and responses of the students to the stories being told to them;
c) check recall of certain elements of each story after it was narrated, with particular focus on the recall of lexical items in rhythmic refrains.

See Appendix 1 (page 26, this volume) for information on the stories used at this stage in the research.

Choice of the experimental story

For the experiment itself, a story to be told purely orally was devised, based upon the contents of a published picture story-book (adapted from the story 'Granny Sticklebeck' by J. Moore and M. Wright). This book was not part of the school book collection and it was therefore safe to say the children had had no previous experience of it. (For the full script of the adapted story see Appendix 2, page 27, this volume.) Nonsense words were used as the focal content of the repeated rhythmic refrain. This was done so that there would be no possibility of the students having heard these words in other contexts in or out of school.

The four nonsense words chosen for the rhythmic refrain section of the story were 'jakus', 'deekans', 'toodles' and 'pollars'. These were specially devised to conform to the phonological possibilities that English allows, and also to have the same number of syllables and the stress placed on the same segment of the word (the first syllable). Because of the importance of creating a meaningful discourse, the context of the story allows them to be interpreted as some sort of tempting sweet or other foodstuff, rather in the way that chocolate bars and other sweets popular with children often have invented names, as in, for example, 'Curly Whirlies' or 'Snickers'. Rhyming words were avoided to ensure that it was only the rhythm and not any rhyme that could be identified as a determining factor for recall.

As mentioned earlier, a finely tuned context helps the learner to infer the meaning of a word. In order that the children would be able to infer the meaning of the nonsense words, a clue was provided in the narrative: the children were told in the story that these were nice things to eat. However, what these particular things were, was left to the imagination of the children. The aim was to see whether these words were spontaneously recalled from the surrounding context when they appeared in a rhythmic section of the story.

Controlling the variables

The story was told in two versions, each to a different group of children (Group A or B) chosen to be comparable in their mix of abilities, as described above.

In each version of the story, only two of the four nonsense words were included in the refrain and the other two were included in the prose narrative. The placement of the pairs of words was reversed between Version A and Version B.

Group A was told the story with the words 'jakus' and 'deekans' in the rhythmic refrain and 'toodles' and 'pollars' in the prose narrative, while Group B was told the story with the words 'toodles' and 'pollars' in the rhythmic refrain and 'jakus' and 'deekans' in the prose narrative.

The number of times each nonsense word was mentioned in the story was the same in each version, i.e. four times in the rhythmic refrain and four times in the prose narrative.

Procedure for narration of the experimental story

From the pilot studies it was observed that after listening to a story once, the children picked up the general gist of the story but not the details. It was therefore decided that the story would be narrated twice.

Before the narration of the story no effort was made to pre-teach the meaning of the unfamiliar words. Nor was there any visual aid to assist the comprehension of the story or the meaning of the words. These aspects of the normal teaching and learning process, although clearly recommendable for normal teaching through stories, were specifically avoided in the experiment in order not to direct attention to any one particular aspect of the story, and thereby raise its prominence, other than by the rhythmic refrain.

The children were allowed to join in with the refrain as it occurred in the story, if this spontaneously occurred, since this was felt to be part of their normal relationship with a story, and one that it would be perverse to exclude even in the controlled conditions of this experiment. The children were not, however, specially 'drilled' or cued to repeat the key rhythmic sections. In fact the amount of this type of spontaneous 'joining in' was equal between the two groups of children.

Collection of data about recall of the 'key' words

As soon as possible after the story had been told, each student met the experimenter individually and was asked the question, 'What did Mrs. Sticklebeck bring for the children?' No other prompting was given. All responses were recorded and noted down. (See Appendix 3.)

Analysis of the results

The results were rather clear cut. In response to the elicitation question, subjects often remembered whole 'chunks' of the story, some of which contained information relevant to the question, some of which did not, but this information on wider recall, which however serves to support the hypotheses on whole 'chunk' recall discussed earlier, was not taken into account for this particular study. Responses are, however, reported verbatim, in full, in Appendix 3 (see page 30), and they are very interesting in themselves, since supposedly familiar content (and thus stressed) words like 'sweets' and 'green' and other, possibly new, stressed content words and rhythmic phrases occurring in the story, like 'ting a ling', form the core of what is recalled.

In addition, we seem to have a number of Young Learners' impositions of commonsense interpretations of 'nice things to eat', that were not actually included in the story, such as 'grapes' and 'crisps', which might be taken to show that they understood the general drift of this new story and were doing their best to fill in the details. It could well be that they had interpreted some of the unknown/nonsense words in ways that made sense to them in the context as names for their favourite snacks (see Donaldson, 1978, for this strong tendency in children to 'make sense' of what they hear). This particular study was not set up to investigate this aspect of children's capacities, but the peripheral results are very suggestive that a study on interpretation of what is recalled could be very worthwhile.

The significant point for this particular study is, however, that where there was verbatim or near-verbatim recall of any of the 'key' nonsense words that were the focus of the study, subjects from both groups spontaneously mentioned words that they had heard in the rhythmic refrain but not from the prose sections of the story. The recall was not always a perfect phonological reproduction of the key words, but the consonant/vowel, and the stress-patterns of the key words were accurately reproduced in the majority of cases.

Statistical analysis of the data

In spite of the apparent clear-cut nature of the results, it had been originally planned to subject the results to statistical analysis, and this procedure was maintained as an additional instrument of analysis. A chi square test was carried out (see page 102 of this volume for an explanation of statistical procedures). The test was chosen for the reasons that nominal data had to be analysed and the numbers involved in the data were small.

Table 1 Recall of 'jakus' and 'deekans'

	At least one recalled	Neither recalled
Group A (jakus and deekans in rhythmic section)	4	8
Group B (jakus and deekans in prose section)	0	12

Table 2 Recall of 'toodles' and 'pollars'

	At least one recalled	Neither recalled
Group A (toodles and pollars in prose section)	0	12
Group B (toodles and pollars in rhythmic section)	6	6

Calculating the significance level for Tables 1 and 2 obtained a significant difference at the 5 per cent and 1 per cent levels, respectively. It can therefore be said that there was a positive association between the ability to recall key words and their appearance in the rhythmic refrain.

However, the numbers in each cell were relatively small. Another test was done combining the results for all the words which were found in the rhythmic refrains.

Table 3 Recall by Groups A and B together

	At least one recalled	Neither recalled
Words in rhythmic section	10	14
Words in prose section	0	24

An association between recall of words and their appearance in the rhythmic refrain was found to be significant at the 1 per cent level.

Discussion of the results

Limitations of the experiment, and recommendations for further research

The numbers of subjects in this experiment were small, and the experiment took place in a particular context, so it is important to interpret these findings with caution. The main study was also undertaken with only one story, so it is difficult to say whether all stories told would evoke the same response. However, the original hypothesis was arrived at through personal experience, and reinforced by the extensive pilot telling of other stories in the experimental situation as a fore-runner to the main experiment. Together, these experiences seemed to support the 'hunch' about rhythm that was the genesis of the study. The experimental story was devised to be very much within a typical genre of repetitive stories with rhythmical elements told orally to children and the very popular picture story-books that are often used by EFL/ESL teachers as a basis for reading aloud to children or 'telling the story with the book'.

The scope of the study was limited, for purely practical reasons, to investigation of recall of newly presented words within a short time after they had been heard in the rhythmic refrain of a story. Although the results were extremely promising in this area, and it might be extrapolated that the normal repetitions that popular stories are given at the request of children over a longer period of time could well lead to a greater long-term uptake of words, and indeed whole 'chunks' of language by many children, this study in itself can make no such claims. Replications of this research through longitudinal studies in the same area could provide some solid data to support or disconfirm this very tempting hypothesis in different Young Learners' situations.

Conclusion

This study, although small-scale, seems to suggest that it is worthwhile for other teachers to follow up the idea with their own students using similar resources, to try to replicate the experiment in a similar 'one-off' fashion, or to perhaps to develop studies of their own to investigate recall and use of salient words found in rhythmic refrains when stories of this type are used over a longer period of time with the repetitions of the story-telling experience that the children not only enjoy but usually demand.

In spite of the fact that the present study was limited to the telling of one story twice but on only one occasion, the results seem indicative that vocabulary elements presented within a rhythmic refrain in a story are more readily recalled by learners than those within the prose narration of a story. It therefore seems that including key words in the rhythmic element of a story is a pedagogic choice which would help to expedite the recall of new words in a target language.

Appendix 1

Examples of story-books containing rhythmic refrains used during the pilot period for this study

Gurney, Nancy and Eric, *The King the Mice and the Cheese* Harper Collins, 1986.
Randall, Ronnie, *The Gingerbread Man* Ladybird Books, 1987.
Stobbs, William, *Chicken Licken* Puffin, 1968.
Sutton, Eve, *My Cat Likes to Hide in Boxes* Puffin, 1978.
Vipont, Elfrida, *The Elephant and the Bad Baby* Hamish Hamilton, 1969.

Appendix 2

Text of the story as told for the experiment, adapted from the story 'Granny Sticklebeck' by J. Moore and M. Wright, Hamish Hamilton, 1981

Version told to Group A: Rhythmic section – jakus and deekans; Prose – toodles and pollars

It was Sunday morning and the children were playing in the park. Suddenly they heard a voice saying,

> Ting-a-ling, ting-a-ling
> Come and see what I have got
> Jakus so sweet and deekans so green.

She had brought all these lovely things for them to eat. When the children heard this, they said, 'That's Mrs Sticklebeck!' and ran to meet her. She had a big bag with lots and lots of things to eat for the children. She showed them the toodles and then she showed them the pollars. She said, 'Come with me and I will give you all this to eat.' The children were very happy and they skipped and ran and followed her. She took them far, far away and no one knew where they had gone.

At eight o'clock the mothers came to the park to take their children home, but there were no children. They were very upset. They went to the police and told them what had happened. The policemen came to the park and searched everywhere but they couldn't find the children. They put up notices saying, 'Children Missing. Help Find Them.'

The next day again some more children were playing in the park and again they heard Mrs Sticklebeck saying,

> Ting-a-ling, ting-a-ling
> Come and see what I have got
> Jakus so sweet and deekans so green.

She had got all these lovely things for them to eat. The children said, 'That's Mrs Sticklebeck!' and ran to meet her. She showed them the toodles and then she showed them the pollars. She said, 'Come with me and I will give you all this to eat.' The children were very happy and they skipped and ran and followed her. She took them far, far away and no one knew where they had gone. Once again the police looked everywhere but they couldn't find the children.

On the third day Mrs Sticklebeck went to another park and said,

> Ting-a-ling, ting-a-ling
> Come and see what I have got
> Jakus so sweet and deekans so green.

She had got all these lovely things for them to eat. Two little boys were playing on the swings. They said, 'That's Mrs Sticklebeck!' and ran to meet her. She showed them the toodles and then she showed them the pollars. She said, 'Come with me and I will give you all this to eat'. The boys followed her and she took them far, far away and no one knew where they had gone.

Again the police came to look for the two boys but couldn't find them.

Now everybody was very frightened. They kept their children at home. They wouldn't let them go to the park. The children said, 'Please, please let us go to the park.' The parents rang up the police to ask them what they should do. The police said, 'Yes, let them go and we'll look after them.' The children were very happy. They ran out to the park and played together. The policemen hid behind the trees and stood there very quiet.

Suddenly they heard a voice saying,

> Ting-a-ling ting-a-ling
> Come and see what I have got
> Jakus so sweet and deekans so green.

She had got all these lovely things for them to eat. The children said, 'That's Mrs Sticklebeck!' and ran to meet her. She showed them the toodles and then she showed them the pollars. She said, 'Come with me and I will give you all this to eat.'

The children were very happy and they ran and skipped and followed her. One by one the policemen came out from behind the trees and caught Mrs Sticklebeck. They said, 'Where are you taking them you horrid woman? Tell us at once.' Mrs Sticklebeck was very frightened. She said, 'Come with me and I'll show you where the children are.' The policemen followed her and they came to her house. All the children were playing there and having fun. Immediately their mothers were called and they were very happy to see their children. They took them home and told them never to run away again.

Version B: Rhythmic section – toodles and pollars; Prose – jakus and deekans

It was Sunday morning and the children were playing in the park. Suddenly they heard a voice saying,

> Ting-a-ling, ting-a-ling
> Come and see what I have got
> Toodles so sweet and pollars so green.

She had brought all these lovely things for them to eat. When the children heard this, they said, 'That's Mrs Sticklebeck!' and ran to meet her. She had a big bag with lots and lots of things to eat for the children. She showed them the jakus and then she showed them the deekans. She said, 'Come with me and I will give you all this to eat.' The children were very happy and they skipped and ran and followed her. She took them far, far away and no one knew where they had gone.

At eight o'clock the mothers came to the park to take their children home, but there were no children. They were very upset. They went to the police and told them what had happened. The policemen came to the park and searched everywhere but they couldn't find the children. They put up notices saying, 'Children Missing. Help Find Them.'

The next day again some more children were playing in the park and again they heard Mrs Sticklebeck saying,

> Ting-a-ling, ting-a-ling
> Come and see what I have got
> Toodles so sweet and pollars so green.

She had got all these lovely things for them to eat. The children said, 'That's Mrs Sticklebeck!' and ran to meet her. She showed them the jakus and then she showed them the deekans. She said, 'Come with me and I will give you all this to eat.' The children were happy and they skipped and ran and followed her. She took them far, far away and no one knew where they had gone. Once again the police looked everywhere but they couldn't find the children.

On the third day Mrs Sticklebeck went to another park and said,

> Ting-a-ling, ting-a-ling
> Come and see what I have got
> Toodles so sweet and pollars so green.

She had got all these lovely things for them to eat. Two little boys were playing on the swings. They said 'That's Mrs Sticklebeck!' and ran to meet her. She showed them the jakus and then she showed them the deekans. She said, 'Come with me and I will give you all this to eat.' The boys followed her and she took them far, far away and no one knew where they had gone. Again the police came to look for the two boys but couldn't find them.

Now everybody was very frightened. They kept their children at home. They wouldn't let them go to the park. The children said, 'Please, please let us go to the park.' The parents rang up the police to ask them what they should do. The police said, 'Yes, let them go and we'll look after them.' The children were very happy. They ran out to the park and played together. The policemen hid behind the trees and stood there very quiet.

Suddenly they heard a voice saying,

> Ting-a-ling ting-a-ling
> Come and see what I have got
> Toodles so sweet and pollars so green.

She had got all these lovely things for them to eat. The children said, 'That's Mrs Sticklebeck!' and ran to meet her. She showed them the jakus and then she showed them the deekans. She said, 'Come with me and I will give you all this to eat.' The children were very happy and they ran and skipped and followed her. One by one the policemen came out from behind the trees and caught Mrs Sticklebeck. They said, 'Where are you taking them you horrid woman. Tell us at once.' Mrs Sticklebeck was very frightened. She said, 'Come with me and I'll show you where the children are.' The policemen followed her and they came to her house. All the children were playing there and having fun. Immediately their mothers were called and they were very happy to see their children. They took them home and told them never to run away again.

Appendix 3

Verbatim responses by subjects asked what they remembered after the second telling of the story of Mrs Sticklebeck

Group A (Rhythmic section – jakus and deekans; Prose – toodles and pollars)

Subject no.	Response
1	Jakus so sweet, deegans so green, police were hiding. Mrs Sticklebeck very scared, follow me and I'll show you. Mum said you mustn't run away.
2	Sweet, don't know.
3	Orange, banana, grapes.
4	Green, sweets, she ring the bell and she came.
5	Jakasu, sweet, jakasu so green, took far away, then the mummies came, put the notice in everyone's house 'children are missing', mummies said 'now what to do', police said 'let them go' police hid, then ting a ling, lady came, jakasu so sweet, green. Then the police said where are the other children. Lady said 'I'll show you' and the lady showed. Then and the children happy playing there.
6	Sweet and green, ting a ling, I've got green and sweet, police came. Can't find them, let them go to the garden, two boys, then the ting a ling, sweet, green.
7	Sweets, gulas, cakes.
8	Ting a ling, ting a ling, spakus so green, they walked and walked, ting a ling, spakus so green, ting a ling, spakus so green.
9	Green, sweet, ting a ling, don't know.
10	Crisps, don't know.
11	–
12	Ting a ling, jackus so sweet, fathers and mothers came, they were upset, then they called the police, then they searched and searched and searched. That's it.

Group B (Rhythmic section – toodles and pollars; Prose – jakus and deekans)

Subject no.	Response
1	Ting a ling, toodles so green.
2	Ting a ling, sweet.
3	Sweet.
4	Ting a ling, see what I've got, pollars, sweet, green.
5	Ting a ling, come and see what I have got, polis.
6	Toodles, sweets, green.
7	Won't tell.
8	Lollipop, sweetie, drink, cola, grapes.
9	Sweet, green, polis.
10	Sweet, ting a ling.
11	Don't know.
12	Ting a ling, chocolate, polchers so green.

3 The Value of Grammatical Information in a Dictionary for Young Learners

Hilary Nesi
*Centre for English Language Teacher Education,
University of Warwick*

One of the major distinctions between dictionaries designed for native speakers and dictionaries designed for non-native speakers is that non-native-speaker dictionaries provide more information about word grammar and use. This difference exists because lexicographers assume that foreign-language learners, unlike native speakers, lack the morphological, syntactic and collocational knowledge to use new words correctly once their meaning is made known. Encoding information may also be more prominent in non-native-speaker dictionaries because English-language learners are expected to use their dictionaries as a writing aid, while native-speaker users are expected to gather mainly receptive knowledge from the dictionary entry. Native speakers have more opportunity to gain full productive knowledge gradually, through a prolonged series of encounters with the same word in a variety of different contexts. This is the 'natural' way to learn new words, but it takes time that most foreign-language learners can ill-afford, hence the attempt on the part of dictionary designers to shortcut the acquisition process and provide all the necessary word information at one sitting.

It remains unclear, however, to what extent a dictionary entry can help language learners acquire productive word knowledge. It is possible that elaborate encoding information confuses learners, and the space it takes up could perhaps be used more profitably in other ways. This consideration is particularly relevant to the design of Young Learners' dictionaries because children are not trained or sophisticated users. Dictionaries could contain more pictures, or be printed in a larger font, if grammatical and morphological information was omitted. Although all primary learners' dictionaries provide less elaborate word information than dictionaries for advanced adult learners there is still great variation in the quantity of grammar and morphology that they contain, and those that offer more must inevitably reduce their provision of other, perhaps more beneficial, features.

The effects of including and excluding grammatical information in the dictionary entry need to be investigated, so that the producers and purchasers of dictionaries can make more informed decisions about the kind of dictionary Young Learners need. Information about the way children use dictionaries is also valuable to teachers, who have to decide how much importance to attach to word class and morphological information when they help children to interpret dictionary entries.

A number of investigations into users' interpretation of different dictionary entry styles have required experimental subjects to read entries for unknown words and then compose sentences containing these new words. The results of these experiments testify to the difficulty of the task. Although in many cases subjects were found to manifest some partial understanding of the meaning, collocation and syntax of the look-up words, these words were nevertheless often used in wildly inappropriate ways.

In studies where young native-speaker dictionary users were required to produce sentences (Mitchell, 1983(a) and 1983(b); Miller and Gildea, 1985, 1987; McKeown, 1991), the dictionary entries were often hard to understand and/or misleading, and their inadequacy may help to account for some of the many errors that the children made. McKeown, for example, found a high rate of unacceptability (75 per cent) in scorable sentences produced after consulting old-style elementary school dictionaries which were essentially abbreviated versions of entries written for adults. However, although scores improved when specially written definitions, judged to be more accessible and less vague, were substituted for the original dictionary entries, the problem of misproduction was by no means solved. Fifty per cent of the sentences scored in McKeown's second experiment, with rewritten definitions, were still judged to be unacceptable.

In studies of adult non-native-speaker dictionary users (Jain, 1981; Black, unpublished but cited in Maingay and Rundell, 1987; Nesi and Meara, 1994; Nesi, 1994), subjects consulted entries from major learners' dictionaries which contained far more morphological, syntactic and collocational information than the entries consulted by the young native speakers. The success rate for the tasks was low, and subjects often generated inappropriate sentences that were remarkably similar to those produced by native-speaker child subjects. Although they were advanced learners of English, many subjects found it difficult to interpret and apply the grammatical information signalled in the entries.

In all these studies subjects were required to have complete control over the unknown word: its meaning, syntax, morphology, collocation and even register. The poor success rate regardless of the completeness of the dictionary entry may simply be a reflection of the difficulty of the task. None of the studies focused on young non-native-speaker dictionary users, but it is reasonable to assume that children working in a foreign language would be even less proficient in processing word information than non-native-speaker adults, or children working in their first language.

The present study was designed to investigate the value of grammatical information (as opposed to information about meaning, collocation and register) in entries for a projected new primary-level learners' dictionary. For this reason non-native-speaker children were used as experimental subjects, and, in order to reduce the demand on other aspects of their productive word knowledge, the main task required them to recognise correct and incorrect structures, rather than to produce their own sentences.

The children were initially required to state how well they knew the words chosen for the experiment. They were then given access to dictionary entries at three levels of grammatical completeness, and were asked to rate how helpful they considered the entries to be. Finally they were tested on their understanding of the morphological and syntactic behaviour of the words.

It was hypothesised that the children would score best for words for which they were given the most grammatical information, and least well for words where little or no grammatical information was available. It seemed likely, however, that they would be more interested in word meaning than in word behaviour. It was therefore hypothesised that they would initially judge entries which only provided definitions and examples to be no less helpful (and possibly more helpful) than grammatically detailed entries.

Experimental procedure

One thousand five hundred subjects from Egypt, Ghana, Jordan, South Africa, Uganda, and Zimbabwe took part in the study. All were children studying in grades 5 and 6 of English medium primary schools (mean age 11.3 years, s.d. .96). The majority of subjects from Egypt and Jordan spoke Arabic at home, whilst those from Ghana, South Africa, Uganda and Zimbabwe spoke African languages. Some subjects claimed to speak two or even three languages at home, including English and/or another European language. The subjects were tested in their own classrooms, under examination conditions. Class teachers supervised the administration of the tests.

Twelve words were used in the study. The words were common enough to include in a Young Learners' dictionary with a core vocabulary of about 2500 words, but they were judged to be relatively difficult words for fifth- and sixth-grade non-native speakers. The words represented different grammatical categories: noun, irregular noun, irregular verb, regular and irregular verb and gradable adjective (see Table 1). Two different sets of words were used to increase the likelihood that some words in each grammatical category would be unknown to the subjects.

Table 1 Words used in Tests A and B

Test A			Test B		
1	**injury**	*noun*	1	**luxury**	*noun*
2	**ox**	*irregular noun*	2	**buffalo**	*irregular noun*
3	**lend**	*irregular verb*	3	**split**	*irregular verb*
4	**freeze**	*irregular verb*	4	**kneel**	*irregular verb*
5	**smell**	*regular and irregular verb*	5	**lean**	*regular and irregular verb*
6	**fierce**	*gradable adjective*	6	**smooth**	*gradable adjective*

Dictionary entries for these 12 words were used to create 12 different versions of a four-stage test. The 12 versions of the test each consisted of a leaflet made from one sheet of A3 paper folded in half, or four sheets of A4 stapled together (the format depended on the photocopying resources of the schools where the tests were administered). The 12 versions of the test were distributed to subjects in roughly equal quantity (see Table 2).

Table 2 Numbers of subjects taking each version of the test

	One	Two	Three	Four	Five	Six	Total
Version A	132	145	136	137	133	133	**816**
Version B	109	118	123	112	121	101	**684**
Total	241	263	259	249	254	234	**1500**

On the front page of each leaflet subjects were asked for personal details (their age and the language(s) they spoke at home) and were also asked to rate their familiarity with the six words on a scale from 1 to 5 (1= I don't know this word at all, 5 = I know this word very well). This page only varied across versions A and B of the test; version A testing subjects' knowledge of **injury**, **ox**, **lend**, **freeze**, **smell** and **fierce**, and version B testing knowledge of **luxury**, **buffalo**, **split**, **kneel**, **lean** and **smooth**. On page 2 of the leaflet the same six words appeared with an accompanying dictionary entry; subjects were asked to rate the helpfulness of each entry on a scale from 1 to 5. This page varied across the 12 versions of the test, because although the order of the head-words and the main part of the dictionary entries remained the same, there were differences in the amount of additional morphological and word class information supplied for each word. For example, in Version One of the test the dictionary entry for word one (**injury** in test A and **luxury** in test B) gave the word class in full but no morphological forms, thus:

> **injury** *noun*
> If you have an injury you have hurt part of your body. *Athletes often have sports injuries. He was taken to hospital with a serious injury to his head.*

While the entry for word six (**fierce** in test A and **smooth** in test B) did not give the word class but gave the morphological forms in full, thus:

> **fierce, fiercer, fiercest**
> If an animal is fierce it is angry and it may attack you. *They were hunting a fierce tiger that had eaten two people from the village.*

On the other hand in Version Two of the test the entries for **injury** and **luxury** provided morphological forms but no word class information, while in Version Six of the test **fierce** and **smooth** occurred with word class information but no forms.

Table 3 shows how the quantity of morphological and word class information was rotated across words in each version of the test.

Table 3 The rotation of conditions in the six versions of tests A and B

	One	Two	Three	Four	Five	Six
Word class in full, no forms	1	2	3	4	5	6
Word class abbreviated, no forms	2	3	4	5	6	1
No word class, no forms	3	4	5	6	1	2
Word class in full, forms in full	4	5	6	1	2	3
Word class abbreviated, forms in full	5	6	1	2	3	4
No word class, forms in full	6	1	2	3	4	5

This rotation of conditions ensured that comparisons of the effect of differing quantities of grammatical and morphological information were not affected by the varying difficulty of head-word meaning.

It should be noted that although the quantity of morphological and word class information was rotated across words, the main part of each dictionary entry also contained a certain amount of grammatical information, and this was available even to subjects operating in the *no word class, no forms* condition. All the entries provided covert word class information, and the entries for **injury**, **luxury**, **ox**, **buffalo**, **lend**, **kneel**, **smell** and **lean** also contained inflected forms. (In the case of **smell** and **lean** only one of the correct alternative past tense forms was given: **smelt** and **leant**, but not **smelled** and **leaned**). It should also be noted that general spelling and grammar rules could be applied to some of the words used in the test. For example anyone conversant with the basic rules of English spelling could deduce that **injuries** was the plural of **injury**, and anyone knowing the grammar and morphology of gradable adjectives would be able to generate **smoother** and **fiercest** from **smooth** and **fierce**. Therefore the additional word form and word class information included in the entries for some words in each test condition tended to have a reinforcing role; reminding the user of general rules, or drawing attention to information also recoverable from context.

On page 3 of the test, subjects were required to mark as right or wrong three sentences for each of the six word categories. In the discussion that follows, the normal convention of preceding an incorrect form with an asterisk (*) will be followed. For the first five word categories (**injury/luxury**, **ox/buffalo**, **lend/split**, **freeze/kneel** and **smell/lean**) sentences one and two required subjects to recognise correct and incorrect word morphologies (**injuries** and ***injurys**; **oxen** and ***oxes**, for example), and question three required subjects to recognise incorrect word class use (for example, *'He didn't want to injury his foot' and *'The cows buffalo in the field'). For the gradable adjective category (**fierce/smooth**) question one required recognition of correct morphology ('This is the fiercest animal in the zoo' and 'Which stone is smoother?'), and questions two and three required recognition of incorrect word class (for example *'A smooth is expensive' and *'This animal fierces me').

Results

The six types of entry can be placed on a cline stretching from the maximally informative *word class in full, forms in full*, to the minimally informative *no word class, no forms*. It is convenient to group these into three levels of condition:

high level of information = 1. Word class in full, forms in full
2. Word class abbreviated, forms in full
middle level of information = 3. No word class, forms in full
4. Word class in full, no forms
low level of information = 5. Word class abbreviated, no forms
6. No word class, no forms

Table 4 shows how the entire population rated each of the five information conditions. The statistical measure used here is the Friedman Two-way ANOVA. (See page 102 of this volume for information on statistical procedures.)

Table 4 Perceived helpfulness of the dictionary entries in the six different conditions (1500 subjects)

	Mean rank
Word class in full, no forms	3.49
Word class abbreviated, no forms	3.49
No word class, no forms	3.45
Word class in full, forms in full	3.49
Word class abbreviated, forms in full	3.54
No word class, forms in full	3.54

A slight preference was indicated for low levels of information (no forms, and abbreviated or no word class), but there was no significant difference in the perceived helpfulness of entries in the six conditions (df 5 significance .7692).

Initially, scores for all 1500 scripts were calculated by simply marking each word as right if the subject had made three correct identifications, and as wrong if one or more sentence had been incorrectly identified. For example, subjects were judged to have the word luxury right if they placed a tick by 'Chocolate and perfume are luxuries' and a cross by *'Chocolate and perfume are luxurys' and *'She didn't want to luxury her children'.

As can be seen from Table 5, entries where the word forms were provided in full resulted in slightly more correct answers. The best results were for words provided with forms in full, but no word class information. The worst results, predictably, were for words provided with no grammatical information at all (no word class, no forms).

Table 5 Scores in the six different conditions (1500 subjects)

	All three recognition tasks correct (%)	One or more recognition tasks correct (%)
Word class in full, forms in full	615 (42.4)	837 (57.6)
Word class abbreviated, forms in full	638 (44.1)	808 (55.9)
No word class, forms in full	650 (44.7)	803 (55.3)
Word class in full, no forms	601 (41.4)	850 (58.6)
Word class abbreviated, no forms	620 (42.5)	838 (57.5)
No word class, no forms	588 (40.7)	855 (59.3)

These results confirm the initial hypothesis that additional grammatical information is not recognised as helpful, but in fact benefits the user in tasks focusing on accuracy. It must be borne in mind, however, that this first analysis does not give very precise information about the potential benefit of grammatical information. The scoring system did not differentiate between subjects who made only one mistake, for example by accepting an incorrect plural form, and subjects who completely misunderstood the grammar of the word. A further problem with the initial marking scheme was that it did not take into account the fact that many subjects knew some of the words already. We might expect dictionary entries for familiar words to be read less carefully than dictionary entries for unfamiliar words. It also seems likely that, in cases where dictionary users know, or think they know, the grammar of a word already, this knowledge supplements or even overrides the information provided in the dictionary.

In order, therefore, to reduce the effect of prior word knowledge on the interpretation of dictionary information, an analysis was made of responses for each word from subjects who rated it at familiarity level one or two (and thus claimed little or no prior knowledge of it). In this analysis far fewer test responses were examined, but because of the large size of the subject population it was possible to obtain a sufficient sample for each word category in each condition. Table 6 shows the number of test responses that were analysed in each condition. It will be seen that certain words proved to be much better known than others. Almost all subjects claimed familiarity with **freeze** and **smell**, for example, whilst **injury**, **luxury**, **ox** and **fierce** were not well known.

These test responses were analysed in much closer detail. Each response to each word in each condition was marked on a scale from 0 (none of the three sentences marked correctly) to 3 (all three sentences marked correctly). Table 7 shows the mean scores for each condition, and reveals that subjects tended to do better when forms and/or word class information were provided in full.

The Kruskal-Wallis one-way ANOVA test indicated significant differences between scores ($p = .004$). The Mann-Whitney test showed no significant differences between scores in conditions at the high and middle information levels, but significant differences ($p = < .05$) between the two high and the two low

Table 6 Numbers of subjects in each condition claiming little or no prior word knowledge

	injury/ luxury	ox/ buffalo	lend/ split	freeze/ kneel	smell/ lean	fierce/ smooth	Total
Word class in full, forms in full	44/66 **110**	39/25 **64**	18/30 **48**	10/20 **30**	2/31 **33**	42/20 **62**	**347**
Word class abbreviated, forms in full	52/68 **120**	39/30 **69**	16/34 **50**	10/18 **28**	4/36 **40**	39/19 **58**	**365**
No word class, forms in full	45/48 **93**	50/27 **77**	11/36 **47**	6/22 **28**	5/35 **40**	35/20 **55**	**340**
Word class in full, no forms	39./53 **92**	42/19 **61**	19/32 **51**	9/24 **33**	4/40 **44**	44/14 **58**	**339**
Word class abbreviated, no forms	35/54 **89**	40/20 **60**	13/33 **46**	7/26 **33**	3/44 **47**	37/22 **59**	**334**
No word class, no forms	36/57 **93**	32/14 **46**	15/22 **37**	6/25 **31**	6/31 **37**	45/24 **69**	**313**
Total	**597**	**377**	**279**	**183**	**241**	**361**	**2038**

Table 7 Mean scores in each condition for subjects with little or no prior word knowledge

	mean	s.d.
Word class in full, forms in full	1.95	.91
Word class abbreviated, forms in full	1.99	.95
No word class, forms in full	1.88	.97
Word class in full, no forms	1.95	.93
Word class abbreviated, no forms	1.78	.96
No word class, no forms	1.79	.94

information levels, and between one of the middle information levels (*word class in full, no forms*) and the two low information levels. (See page 102 of this volume for more information on statistical measures.)

Subjects claiming little or no prior word knowledge produced more correct answers than incorrect answers for almost every question in every condition. This seems to suggest that some subjects were able to apply grammatical and morphological rules to some unknown words even when the dictionary entries did not overtly signal the necessary information. In many cases, however, the number of correct answers failed to reach significance level (using the chi-square test, p = < .05), and in these cases it is not safe to ascribe correct answers to anything other than random variation. (See page 102 of this volume for more information.)

Cases where the number of correct answers did reach significance level help to indicate whether or not additional grammatical and morphological information was useful. For example, significantly more subjects in every condition were able to recognise that **injuries** and **luxuries** were correct plural forms, and that ***injurys** and ***luxurys** were incorrect. In order to get the answers right subjects may have applied general rules regarding the plural of nouns ending in -y, but they may also have used the morphological information contained within the example sentences for **injury** and **luxury**: 'Athletes often have sports injuries' and 'They cannot afford luxuries'.

Whatever the strategy employed, it is clear that subjects could manage without the additional morphological information provided in the high information conditions. Significant numbers of subjects in all conditions also marked as correct 'This is the fiercest animal in the zoo' and 'Which stone is smoother?' The comparative and superlative forms do not occur in the entries for **fierce** and **smooth**, so this suggests that subjects could apply general rules for the formation of comparative and superlative adjectives without any additional help from the dictionary entry.

The inflections of **injury**, **luxury**, **fierce** and **smooth** are productive, predictable, and (apart from the slight variation in the -ies inflection) regular in their spoken and written forms. The results suggest that there would be little justification for listing in the final version of the dictionary the inflected forms of words that inflect in this way.

On the other hand recognition of incorrect word class use in *"She didn't want to luxury her children' and *"He didn't want to injury his foot' seemed to depend much more on access to additional dictionary entry information. Significantly more subjects judged these sentences to be wrong in the high information conditions (*word class in full, forms in full* and *word class abbreviated, forms in full*) but significance level (p = < .05) was not reached in the other conditions.

Table 8 shows how results for individual words were spread across all six conditions. Asterisks in this case mark the questions in each condition which significantly more subjects got right rather than wrong. The statistical measure used here was the chi-square test, p = < .05. It will be seen that results for the least well-known words reached significance level more often. This may be because more responses were analysed for these words, and thus a smaller degree of difference between scores in each condition was necessary to prove non-random variation.

The tendency for scores to reach significance level in the high and medium information conditions rather than the low information conditions is evident in Table 8, although the pattern is not entirely consistent, and the condition *no word class, no forms* is slightly more successful than its fellow low information condition *word class abbreviated, no forms*. There is no obvious explanation for this discrepancy, although it is possible that the total absence of additional information encouraged subjects to search the main part of the dictionary entry more closely for clues regarding word class and morphology.

Results for **ox/buffalo** and **lend/split** provide some evidence to suggest that incorrect word class use is more likely to be recognised when word class information is provided in full, rather than in an abbreviated form.

Results for **freeze/kneel** and **smell/lean** suggest that many subjects were failing to benefit from even the highest levels of grammatical information; nevertheless scores that reached significance level did so in the high and medium information conditions rather than the low information conditions. The inflections for these words are rather less productive, regular and predictable, and it may be that they will have to be flagged more conspicuously in the dictionary entry in order to alert users to their deviation from the regular pattern.

Table 8   Results reaching significance level in each of the six conditions

question number	injury/ luxury 1 2 3	ox/ buffalo 1 2 3	lend/ split 1 2 3	freeze/ kneel 1 2 3	smell/ lean 1 2 3	fierce/ smooth 1 2 3
Word class in full, forms in full	* * *	– – *	* – *	– * –	* – –	* * *
Word class abbreviated, forms in full	* * *	* – *	* * *	– – –	– – *	– * *
No word class, forms in full	* * –	– – *	* – *	– – –	– – –	* * *
Word class in full, no forms	* * –	* – *	* – *	– – –	* – –	* – *
Word class abbreviated, no forms	* * –	– – –	– – –	– – –	– – –	* – *
No word class, no forms	* * –	– – *	* – *	– – –	– – –	* * –

Conclusion

Overall this study confirmed the hypothesis that the children would achieve higher scores on grammar recognition tasks when provided with higher levels of grammatical information. It also confirmed the hypothesis that the children would not perceive more grammatically detailed entries to be more helpful. This second finding incidentally supports the method of data-gathering adopted in this study. Results from a questionnaire-based survey would have almost certainly failed to reveal the value of grammar information in the dictionary entries, because respondents were not aware themselves of the benefit they derived from this kind of information.

In their discussion of the way readers at different levels of morphological awareness understand word families, Bauer and Nation (1993) criticise the inconsistent treatment of derived forms in dictionaries, and propose that within the dictionary entry inflections and affixes should be treated in a more principled and consistent way. This study is an attempt to gauge the amount of grammatical information to be provided in a primary level learners' dictionary by testing potential users' response to sample entries. Although overall the findings matched initial expectations, the interpretation of some responses is not entirely clear, and the experiment did not completely resolve the question of what to include and what to leave out of a dictionary entry. The recommendation is, however, that dictionaries for Young Learners in this age group should contain full word class information for all words, and full forms of less regular and predictable inflections. Inevitably some users will find this information unnecessary, and others will find it insufficient, but the decision is principled and consistent, and is supported by the evidence from this study.

Acknowledgements

Gill McLean, Commissioning Editor at Macmillan Education Ltd, was responsible for the distribution and collection of the tests described in this paper. We would both like to thank the principals, class teachers and pupils of the forty primary schools that took part in the study.

4 Enchantment in the Classroom: Children's Literature as a Teaching Aid

Piotr Kuhiwczak
*Centre for British and Comparative Cultural Studies,
University of Warwick*

In this article children's literature is broadly defined as reading matter and any accompanying illustrations that are available to young children, including picture-books, comics, books of verse and illustrated information books. The article looks at children's literature from the point of view of the cultural and ideological messages it can carry, whether or not this is intentional on the part of the authors. When literature from another culture is used as one aspect of teaching language, it is advisable for teachers not only to pay attention to the linguistic content, but also to be aware of the potential difficulties and opportunities offered by its cultural 'strangeness'. To illustrate this 'strangeness effect' a number of examples are given from children's literature originating from countries such as Poland, Germany and Romania, where translation into English has not resolved all the questions of meaning for readers who do not share the cultural background of the original audience. The reader is invited to reflect on whether the content and assumptions of some of the children's literature chosen to support EYL teaching might bring similar perplexities and opportunities.

It is rarely the case that professionals want to consider the validity of a layman's view on any particular subject, even if the outcome of their professional discussion is going to affect a wide segment of the population. Although I cannot pretend to be entirely ignorant about the issues of language teaching, because I was trained as a teacher and did a short stint at a secondary school, the fact is I have not visited a language classroom for quite a while. In my defence, however, my professional preoccupation with the issues of translation and inter-cultural transfer have provided me with a better understanding of the interaction between the texts and their readers. There are also two personal reasons why I have dared to contribute to this volume. The first is my personal experience, as somebody who has both learned and thought about languages as well as lived in more than one language and culture. The second is the experience of my children who are being brought up in a bilingual family, and educated in the very multicultural and multilingual environment of an inner city school. It is the education of my children in particular that provokes interesting thoughts about the role of children's literature in personal development and language acquisition.

Children's literature as an academic field

Although we all agree that literature plays a significant role in the development of a child, it is only recently that literature for children has been given public status and attracted serious critical attention. This does not mean that previously children were left with their books on their own. The case was just the opposite – until recently children's reading has been a matter of strict familial control and books for children were considered to be a *natural* channel through which approved values were transmitted to the younger generation. The didactic aspects of the texts had primacy over the aesthetic ones, and the only way a child could escape such control was through unsupervised access to the parents' bookshelves. The fact that children's literature has become part of the public domain, is due both to social and technological changes.

Today, texts are available in a variety of ways, and both social and parental control over what children read, watch and listen to has become difficult to sustain. It is also clear that, in a liberal society, there is no one set of moral values on which we all agree. The difficulty with supervising what children read and watch has had both positive and negative effects, and the invasion of visual material has in many cases undermined children's ability to concentrate on printed texts. But it seems to me that this moral and technological deregulation has brought more gains than losses. First of all, the competitive environment has forced the publishers to take children seriously as consumers of books. Secondly, the fact that literature for children has become an object of study means that there is a chance that this knowledge can have some impact on how we deal with it both at home and at school.

Children's literature and learners of foreign languages

The use of literary texts in foreign language teaching has a long history. No need here to refer to the traditional methods by which classical languages have been taught until very recently. But literature has played an important role in teaching modern European languages as well, and some teachers of modern languages at a tertiary level are still convinced that the best method of teaching a foreign language is through reading canonical literary texts. The debate about the place of literature in teaching language skills is far from settled, and contemporary authors of language teaching manuals propose different solutions. I shall not dwell on these debates here, because they usually deal with either teenage or adult learners who are supposed to have some training in reading literary texts. The issue I want to address here is the role of literary texts in teaching very young learners, for whom subtle theoretical distinctions do not make much sense, but who seem to enjoy literature none the less and more than their older brothers and sisters. Since it is neither possible nor desirable to cover this field in a short article, I shall look only at a few aspects, such as the choice of texts, and their linguistic and cultural suitability for educational purposes.

There is no doubt in my mind that teaching a foreign language to Young Learners is a much more difficult proposition than teaching an older constituency. The main problems, of course, are attention span and motivation. Anyone who has taught at primary school understands the problem too well, but outsiders tend to think that difficulties with school children begin later. Keeping a group of 20 or 36 seven-year-olds in reasonable order for 40 intellectually productive minutes is a major achievement, and conveying the message about the importance of learning a foreign language borders on the miraculous. But it is already at this initial point of our discussion that we encounter cultural problems, because it is not true that the task of teaching a foreign language is the same everywhere.

There is no doubt that the problems with attention and motivation depend on many factors, but what we can be sure about is that it is much easier to teach English to children in Poland or Switzerland, than German to children in Britain or the United States. The reason is simply basic motivation on the part of both pupils and their parents, not to mention the teachers. For children who live, for example, in the Midlands of England and spend their holidays in places where many people speak English anyway, and for the rest of the year have access to twenty cable channels with English-language broadcasts, to learn German seems like a perverse form of torture. For the Poles or the Swiss, however, who from a very early age realise that their native languages are not widely spoken and who may watch some of the same television programmes as children in the Midlands, it is clear that English must be the language both of power and fun, since all the Disney characters speak English.

Whatever the initial cultural set-up is, it is clear that every language teacher will have to think seriously about how the available teaching aids may help him/her make the teaching environment attractive and learning desirable. As Collie and Slater (1994:6) rightly put it, 'one primary factor to consider is, we suggest, whether a particular work is able to stimulate the kind of personal involvement ... by arousing the learners' interest and provoking strong, positive reactions from them.' This, I would say, is a preliminary condition any teacher will have to take on board, but there are more specific ones I would like to look at.

One of the reasons why literature may be of use in the classroom at an early stage is because of its authenticity. The concept is perceived as value loaded (Kramsch, 1994), but it seems to me that one can be more relaxed about it at this early stage. As research in child psychology has shown, one of the biggest differences between older and younger children is that younger children do not cope very well with abstractions. They master more easily what is concrete and tangible. This explains, of course, why publishers take so much trouble to make books for children visually attractive, and why so much attention is paid to detail. So at the early stage if a book attracts a child's attention in one way or another, this interaction already sets up an authentic relationship.

Quite often it is curiosity which arrests a child's attention for a moment. Unlike standard international paperbacks, books for children still carry a distinct local flavour. This may be a peculiar graphic design, the format, or something as simple as the quality of paper and print. For instance, it is easy even for a child to realise that many American books look somehow more luxurious than the British ones, while the East European tradition of book illustration is also different from what is acceptable in Britain and the United States. Novelty and strangeness have their own value, and children tend to believe that the grass is greener elsewhere. Thus while our children may value East

European graphic design for its high quality, East European publishers tell us that their readers want more 'Western' photographic realism, because this is what they associate with the better, more technologically advanced world.

Difference and 'strangeness' in children's literature

But although the visual and tactile quality of the book helps to keep the young interested, it is not sufficient to turn a literary text into a teaching aid. There are more substantial issues. One of the major ones is cultural difference. In recent years the cultural aspects of language teaching have been widely discussed. Some authors, like Mike Byram, for instance have looked at this problem in the context of European integration (Byram and Morgan, 1994). Too often, however, the discussion concentrates on older learners who can cope with the issue of cultural difference in a much more conscious and explicit way than young children. It is also the case that the suggested strategies for teaching language and culture are discussed in the context of goals which are supposed to be achieved, such as cultural awareness and inter-cultural mediation. What often eludes the discussion is the point at which learners begin their inter-cultural quest. It seems to me that teaching Young Learners provides a unique opportunity to see how cultural clichés and prejudices arise and what cultural baggage learners bring with them to the classroom. The reason for this transparency is simple – unlike adults, children are on the whole uninhibited and unselfconscious.

Literature for children is a good source of information about cultural values, because it tells us what adults want children to believe, so through books for children we learn about deeply ingrained cultural habits. The 'political correctness' movement or cultural revisionism in relation to literature for children only makes these habits more conspicuous, since it reveals to the outsiders what a given society is particularly obsessed with. The degree of political correctness also tells us a lot about the level of adult self-delusion, since children are quite capable of noticing that the non-violent, non-sexist and non-racist world of their book does not exactly represent the world they live in. A good example of what one could easily do without in literature for children, is a small book entitled *How Does a Czar Eat Potatoes?* in which the affluent life of the czar is contrasted with the extreme poverty of the peasants. In visual terms the contrast is highlighted by the fact that the pages about the peasants are in black and white, and those devoted to the czar are in attractive colours. To make sure that the ideological message is not lost on the young reader, a short introduction is supplied in which the 'correct reading' is made explicit:

> How is a czar different from a peasant father? A czar is rich, has extravagant tastes, and cries with other people's tears. A peasant is poor, takes what comes, and cries from his own pain. The contrasts are made from a child's view – a child who knows a father and can but imagine a czar. The verses are wryly humorous; the message is poignant.

The assumption is that the child should sympathise with the peasant, condemn the czar, and perhaps come up with a revolutionary solution to the problem of

Enchantment in the Classroom: Children's Literature as a Teaching Aid   47

© Horst Eckert

© Horst Eckert

Figure 1 Contrasting illustrations from *How does a Czar Eat Potatoes?*

social inequality. This scenario is very unlikely, since for the majority of American and Western European children both the czar and the peasant belong to the world of fairy tales. We may also doubt whether the book encourages stronger responses from children in less affluent regions. But political manipulation in children's literature is not the biggest problem we may encounter. More alarming are cases where writers display their prejudices and ignorance without being aware that, without reference to reality, children may actually absorb negative stereotypes. In *Pollypocket*, a popular magazine for girls, I have come across the following passages on Egypt and Russia, respectively:

> The people of Egypt are divided between two types of cultures. Some are very traditional and prefer to travel by donkey and get their water from the river. Others, are more like you and me – driving in cars and living in comfortable bricked (*sic!*) flats and houses. The languages spoken by Egyptian people are English, French and Arabic.

> Russia is famous for its beautiful churches. They are decorated with brightly-coloured pictures and lovely golden ornaments. Lots of Russian buildings have funny, onion-shaped roofs called minarets – you will be amazed!

Cross-cultural tensions

But cultural difference is not always a matter of such ignorance and insensitivity. More often one comes across a subtle incompatibility of attitudes and values. For instance, it is noticeable that the majority of writers for children in the English-speaking world promote liberal values: straightforward discipline and parental authority are replaced with intricate negotiations. Metaphor and humour are often used as devices to dilute conflicts and to deal with conflicts and fears, as in *The Magic Lavatory* and *My Mother is Weird*. However, this tradition is not universal and as a result not all English books for children travel equally well. Sometimes a book gets culturally adjusted just after crossing the English Channel:

> There are numerous French translations of English children's books (for instance, French editions of Roald Dahl) that attempt to match TTs [target text] to ST [source text] expectations. Yet, significantly, translations of English children's books into French never seem to follow a strategy of cultural adaptation to expectations *higher* than those placed on their ST readership, whereas many TTs are manifestly adapted to *lower* expectations. There is reason to believe, in fact, that English children's literature is stereotypically perceived as being too 'adult' for a young French readership. (Hervey, 1997:61)

A similar clash between source and target value systems occurred in Poland when Dahl's books were introduced a few years ago. Despite good translations and an advertising campaign co-ordinated by the publishers with the showing of the film version of *Matilda*, none of Dahl's books has sold well. Reviewers point to the anti-authoritarian streak in Dahl's books as the main reason why Polish parents decide to stick to *Winnie-the-Pooh* and *Anne of Green Gables*. Hervey admits that he has no sociological evidence to support his findings, but it seems that the difficulty in promoting Dahl in these two countries cannot be explained as a coincidence. There is no doubt that Poland's traditional literature for children differs from Britain's. While there seems to be a strong tendency in England to encourage a child's independence at a very early stage, the Polish tradition has been to protect children from the outside world for as long as possible. Perhaps in this respect, France is located somewhere between Poland and England and this is reflected in the way the French 'moderate' English books through translation. It is certainly conspicuous that British and American writers tend to play down the importance of adults, and strongly emphasise the child's independence. A number of literary devices have been developed to lift the controlling power of adults. When the adults are temporarily removed, the world changes its usual shape: strange characters appear (*The Cat in the Hat*) and animals acquire human qualities (*Skip to My Lou*). If the plot does not make it easy for the writer to get rid of adults altogether, then dream convention or magic are deployed as in *Where the Wild Things Are* or in *The Magic Lavatory*.

But the British ambivalence about childhood, reflected also in the writing for adults – *Lord of the Flies* being a prime example – is in contrast to attitudes in other countries. Alexander Herzen, for instance, interestingly expressed the Russian attitude to childhood, which has not changed that much since his time: 'We think that the purpose of the child is to grow up because it does grow up. But its purpose is to play, to enjoy itself to be a child. If we merely look to the end of the process, the purpose of all life is death.' (Herzen, 1994) Italian attitudes seem to be similar, if we accept Tim Parks' analysis of contemporary Italian society in *An Italian Education* (Parks, 1996). Allowing children to remain children for as long as possible, however, has its side effects. One of them is the overwhelming presence of adult values. This is not necessarily reflected as a traditional discipline but rather as uninspiring didacticism. It becomes striking when some of these texts get translated into English, showing why there may be problems with selling children's books in translation. Let us look at a couple of examples.

The first poem, 'Poor Pussy' was translated in 1988 from Polish.

Poor Pussy

Poor Pussy was sick and lay moaning in bed.
Dr Cat came to him: How are you? he said.
Pussy held out his paw: I'm terribly ill.
Now let me examine you; try to keep still.
The doctor looks grave: What a little glutton;
Didn't stick to mice, but ate pork chops and mu
Very bad... there's fever. Dr Cat shakes his head
The only remedy is a long spell in bed.
On a diet, of course; gruel, no meat.
No ham or sausage and above all, nothing swee
Not a single mouse? Don't be absurd!
Not even a drumstick from a tiny bird?
God forbid! A diet and leeches for sure.

© *Interpress Publishers, Warsaw*

On that depends the success of my cure.
Poor Pussy lay in bed: he'd had a good fright.
No more puddings or pies; mice a distant delight.
He'd been too greedy. Gluttony is a sin.
So he was severely punished, poor thing.
This could be your fate, so children, take heed
And ask the good Lord to preserve you from Greed.
            (*The Flying Cow*, 1988)

The poem rhymes and reads relatively well. Unfortunately, the regular rhyme is assumed to be sufficient reason for children to love the book. If the publishers had tried this poem on a target reader they would have quickly discovered that the translation was a waste of effort. At best 'Poor Pussy' could be considered as a pastiche of a Victorian poem – heavy on didacticism and patronising. No English child would probably be bothered to look at this poem twice. One wonders whether post-1989 children in Poland are still fed this diet?

THE CABBAGE

You are wearing no end of petticoats,
some fuller, others tighter,
all gathered at the waist.
You would never take them off.
You are so proud and puffed up
that you've forgotten all about the garden.
Rather than standing riveted to the ground,
you had better go into the kitchen,
take off your brand-new clothes
and make some meat balls
rolled in cabbage leaves.
What then?

Figure 2   © *Ion Creanga Publishing House, Bucharest*

FASTIDIOUS DOLLIE

Today I've asked a fastidious dollie to lunch.
"Have some cheese pancakes!"
"No, I won't."
"Or some pressed cheese!"
"No, I won't! Take it away."
"Won't you have a jam-roll?"
"No, I won't! It isn't good!"
With such a fastidious dollie
all the food was left on the table.

Figure 3 © *Ion Creanga Publishing House, Bucharest*

The illustrated poems shown here were originally written in Romanian and published in English as *The Tales of a Furry Friend*. They are also a cultural and translation failure, but a more complex one.

What seems to be happening here (see Figure 2, page 50) is that the cat gives a rebuke to the cabbage, represented metaphorically as a female character. The very tone of the monologue is very puzzling and the last phrase 'What then?' leaves one wondering what the poem is exactly about, and why the cat should be so hostile towards the cabbage. If we assume that the poem and the picture constitute a metaphor, then we have further problems to deal with. The cabbage figure is holding a live piglet on the platter, while the cat tells her to go to the

Figure 4 Mit dieser Ampel zeigst du an, wer warten muß, wer fahren kann.   © *Erhard Dietl*

kitchen and make some meat balls rolled in cabbage leaves. There is no doubt that to the Romanian reader the 'transformation' of the piglet into meat balls must be a natural and logical process. It is also clear that the source-text readers must take naturally to the fact that the cabbage character should be a woman, who after being rebuked will go to the kitchen and prepare a tasty meal. One can easily see there is scope for a clash between the cultural messages of this text, and what Anderman calls the learners' 'internal models of the world'. (Anderman and Rogers, 1997).

The next poem (see Figure 3, page 51) is a reworking of a potentially psychologically interesting situation. The child takes over the role of the hostess and the titular 'dollie' is a child invited to lunch. If one of the purposes of the child's play is to deal with the adult world through the imaginative reconstruction of the real situation, then this poem is about discipline. The 'dollie' is a child refusing to eat, and the hostess's only preoccupation is to make sure that her guest is well fed. To any East European reader the scene will be familiar, since it is customary to find Polish, Russian or Jewish mothers thrusting vast amounts of food on their children. The illustration in which the mother exudes considerable authority, mainly because of her size, leaves no doubt that in the source culture the 'mother' is a figure of ultimate authority. But in cultures where food is not an issue of such importance, the poem will remain a mystery. The linguistic incompetence of the translator contributes to the misunderstanding because one can well sympathise with the dollie who is expected to consume a lunch consisting of cheese pancakes, 'pressed' cheese and a jam-roll.

Although it is not likely that teachers of Young Learners will be using translations for teaching purposes, it is through translation that we can most effectively identify the difference between cultural prototypes and how they are fitted, or 'framed' into grammatical categories. As Anna Wierzbicka has shown in her book (1997), cultural difference is often a matter of the vast semantic difference between seemingly simple and commonly used words like bread, friendship and freedom. The fact that these words have formal equivalents in most languages does not mean that the equivalents are functional, and that they represent the same social and cultural reality which is conveyed by the original word. In practice it means that while selecting books a teacher needs to be aware of the messages a simple text may send to Young Learners. A cheerful-looking and well-designed German book *Die Ampel* (Dietl and Andresen, 1987) may look like wonderful material for teaching expressions connected with road traffic (see Figure 4), but its very explicit didactic agenda may reinforce an already existing British stereotype of Germans as a nation obsessed with rules and regulations.

Language level and conceptual level

The issues of semantics bring us to the general question of how appropriate books for children are for teaching a foreign language. One anxiety teachers commonly express is that there is bound to be a mismatch between the learners' intellectual development, their foreign language skills and the age bracket for which the book was originally intended. As a result learners may find themselves working with texts which are linguistically complex but not challenging enough intellectually. Indeed, situations like this may occur. However, it is not uncommon to see native readers enjoying books which were not intended for their particular age bracket. We all know that not all children who learn to read in their first language achieve the same results within the same period of time, and the gap between the child's ability to read and his or her general intellectual development may arise in a first, or native, language context. Additionally, certain books acquire a particular significance in a child's life, and the relatively simple text may be re-read for many years; it is not a secret that many adults derive genuine pleasure from reading books for children, either.

There is no solution to this problem other than good access to a whole range of texts. Some books are so visually attractive that the illustrations will compensate for either linguistic simplicity or difficulty. Books like the 'Spot' series can be used as a ready-made aid for teaching specific grammatical constructions – such as questions. Dr Seuss' books are excellent for teaching colours and numbers, while Pieńkowski's pop-up books may fulfil multiple tasks. Another good way of introducing children to foreign books is through the mix of familiar and unfamiliar. This can be achieved through the available rewritings of fairy tales. What makes the teacher's task easier in this case is the fact that the archetypal story will be known to children, which should make linguistic recognition easier. Fairy tales are particularly interesting because there are usually several versions of the same story available. Different versions of 'Red Riding Hood', for instance, will provide additional excitement because of the way 'rewriters' try to by-pass the problem of killing the wolf, and there is no doubt that here Roald Dahl's version from *Revolting Rhymes* will appeal to children most, because it is both hilariously funny and has a regular rhyme pattern useful for easy memorisation and a role play. The pedagogical possibilities are almost unlimited, and a good teacher should not have difficulty in persuading the school authorities that spending money on authentic literature for children is a good investment in the quality of teaching.

Appendix

Children's literature referred to in text
Allan, N., *The Magic Lavatory* Random House, 1994.
Bernard Westcott, N., *Skip to My Lou* Little Mammoth, 1989.
Dahl, R., *Matilda* Puffin, 1989.
Dahl, R., *Revolting Rhymes* Jonathan Cape, 1982.
Dietl, E. and Andresen, U., *Die Ampel* Ravensburger Buchverlags Otto Maier GmbH, 1987.
Dr Seuss, *The Cat in the Hat* Random House, 1985.
Gilmore, R. and Jones, B., *My Mother is Weird* Ragweed Press, 1995.
Hill, E., *Where's Spot?* Puffin, 1983.
Jackowicz, S., 'Poor Pussy' from *The Flying Cow* Interpress Publishers, Warsaw, 1988.
Milne, A.A., *Winnie-the-Pooh* Methuen, 1926.
Montgomery, L. M., *Anne of Green Gables* Harrap, 1925.
Pieńkowski, J., *Little Monsters* Orchard, 1986.
Pollypocket 1997, 44, and *Pollypocket* 1998, 48.
Rose, A., *How Does a Czar Eat Potatoes?* Abelard-Schuman, 1973.
Sendak, M., *Where the Wild Things Are* Puffin Books, 1970.
Tomescu, V., *The Tales of a Furry Friend* Ion Creanga Publishing House, 1977.

5 Where Do the Words in EYL Textbooks Come From?

Shelagh Rixon
*Centre for English Language Teacher Education,
University of Warwick*

Vocabulary in coursebooks

This study is concerned not so much with how children actually learn vocabulary as with what we can extrapolate about present methodology from commonly accepted ways of packaging it for them in teaching materials. I have deliberately chosen the 'frozen' medium of textbook writing precisely because it is just that: the evidence, fixed on the page, of what a professional course-provider planned and executed, presumably in the best way that he or she could.

This presentation of vocabulary on the page is, of course, at several removes from what is made of it in the interaction between teacher and pupils when the materials take on their classroom life. However, for many teachers a textbook is the syllabus starting-point and the vertebral column of much teaching. Writers' decisions about vocabulary presentation could fairly be studied as evidence of current approaches to the subject that are likely to be communicated to teachers through their acquaintance with particular textbooks.

I chose seven internationally available textbooks from six different British publishing houses, all used in state primary-level schools and private language schools in many countries. All are intended for a first year of beginners learning English from about the age of eight with a target number of approximately 90 hours, and all have been published within the last ten years. My experience with primary teachers of English has been that they tend to regard such books as 'about the same', preferring one over the other for reasons that may not give their linguistic content as much weight as other criteria, such as quality of illustrations, interest of topic or of story line and types of activity. For the purposes of contrast, I also looked at a much older book, L.G. Alexander's *Look, Listen and Learn!* (1968).

My aim was not to evaluate or make invidious comparisons amongst the books, but rather to uncover evidence of consensus or divergence, and to find some neat ways of doing so that would not require scanning or computing facilities beyond the reach of most teachers or researchers who might want to do something similar with the same or other books. See Appendix 4 (page 71, this volume) for a list of the books analysed. As far as possible, I have avoided identifying individual books in the tables and discussion that follow.

Comparing book with book

A comparison of the vocabulary treatment in the books studied proved far from simple to carry out. This is for the perhaps understandable reason that a textbook is not intended as a direct illustration to the academic world of a credo or of the writer's rationale, but as a practical support to teachers' work. Thus, much of the thinking and planning becomes imbedded, even buried, in the materials on the page. In the teachers' books that accompany these courses, authors tend to be rather silent on the subject of the selection and ordering of the language content of their syllabuses and they say particularly little about vocabulary in this regard.

There are differences over where the information about vocabulary content is given, and by implication for whom it is intended. Alphabetically ordered lists of words for pupils are supplied in some cases, but it is also common practice to provide a list of words organised according to topic in another place in the pupils' book. This is sometimes, but not always, supplemented by a separate, often longer, list of words for the teacher's information in the teacher's book. Policies also differ over whether words are 'signalled' to the teacher as being for productive or receptive use. Although some books are quite specific:

> This is a complete list of both the productive AND receptive words in *Buzz* for YOUR OWN REFERENCE. It includes all the instruction words and many, many words the pupils don't need either to use or to learn. ...There's also a lesson-by-lesson list of productive words on page 120.

Others say little or nothing on the subject, or simply put the label P or R next to the word. The meaning, in pedagogic rather than 'pious-hope' terms, of 'productive' and 'receptive' must be the subject of another research project. For the present study, in all cases, I chose to analyse the longer list where different ones were provided for teachers and pupils, and, because of the uncertainty over exactly what productive and receptive signified for each course, ignored the distinction and included all the words that were offered as part of the course.

Different publishers and authors adopt different 'house styles' and different lexicographical policies about how to present even something as seemingly uncontroversial as a word list. In some courses, all categories of word are listed as vocabulary items, including articles, demonstratives, pronouns and separate inflexions of some verbs, e.g. 'be' and 'have'. In others, there is strict adherence to head-words only as items. This made the first aim – a simple comparison of the numbers of lexical items present in the different courses, followed by an analysis of which items were common ground for most courses – less simple to achieve than might have been expected.

In order to reduce this varied presentation of information to something from which valid comparisons could be made, it was necessary to adopt procedures so that like could be compared with like. Firstly, I decided what words to delete or to conflate under a single head-word. For the purposes of the study, grammar items such as articles, determiners and pronouns were excluded, after a check that they were indeed present in all courses, whether or not they were contained in the word list of any particular book. I felt that it was necessary to some extent to override the distinction between full lexical items (full verbs, adverbs, nouns and adjectives) and grammar items by keeping in items such as prepositions which carry enough meaning for most teachers to want to see them on vocabulary lists. For the purposes of this study, inflections such as plural forms were not counted as separate items; even the irregular plurals such as 'teeth' were counted in with the head-word as the same item. The inflections of 'be' were not counted as different items.

Items from lexical sets, such as days of the week, numbers, countries and months were taken into consideration and listed as part of the study. In fact some coursebooks did not include them in their 'public' lists of words in the course but they were to be found in the text of the lessons. On the final inventory I ignored the days and months and counted only the numerals one to thirty in full series as separate items. Where some courses continued with the number system (up to one hundred in two of the courses) I followed the word lists in giving only the items 'forty', 'fifty', etc. Phrasal verbs, and formulaic phrases such as 'what's the matter?' were also included as single vocabulary items on my list, where one or more of the textbooks had included them. The reader might not agree with all of my decisions, but, I can say with some asperity after disentangling the information from the different books, at least I have made them transparent!

The list of words arrived at was stored on a spreadsheet, using the MicroSoft Works program. This was convenient since it easily allowed new items to be inserted in alphabetical order as they were collected, book by book, but the length of the list did cause some memory problems, at least on my computer. See Appendix 1 for a sample printout.

Results

An inventory was thus arrived at containing 889 separate vocabulary items present in one or more of the seven textbooks under study. The range of total vocabulary items for individual books went from 181 to 459.

Results are shown in the bar chart in Figure 1.

This range of totals was wide, but there is nothing here that allows us to make any evaluative comment on which author's policy about quantity of vocabulary seems the most well founded. It could well be that there is a trade-off in some books in which perhaps a lower level of vocabulary inclusion is balanced by concentration on the development of a large number of grammatical structures, or the converse might be the case – high vocabulary, lower concentration on grammar development. There is also the possibility of low vocabulary with low focus on grammatical development or high vocabulary, high grammatical development. This should be the subject of another study. What can certainly be said, however, is that teachers need to be aware that similar-looking books may contain considerably different ingredients and modes of presenting them.

The question of what is the most reasonable target vocabulary for a first-year beginners' course for children of about 8 years old, or for any other type of young learner for that matter, is obviously not answerable without information on a particular situation, most effectively supported by reports of actual

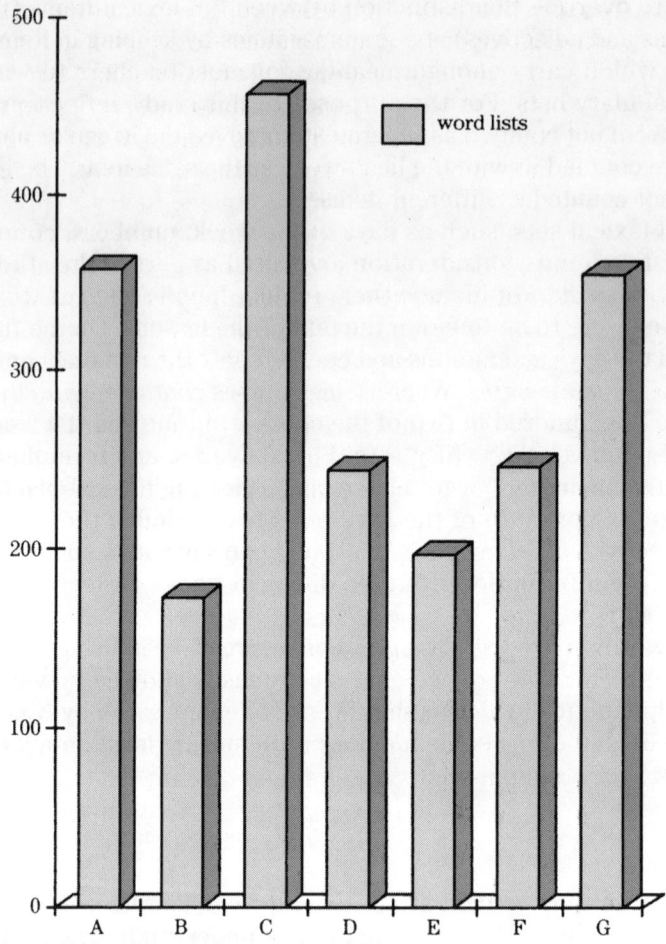

Figure 1 Number of vocabulary items in each of seven books

children's achievements over past years, and without closer consideration of what it means to 'know' vocabulary. However, the fact remains that these seven books seem to embody very different views of what is a reasonable target to present to children in a first-year beginners' course. 'How many words?' is not the sort of question that seems to be in the front line of priority in the 1990s, when the focus of interest has largely shifted from the *content* of language teaching to the *approaches* and *methods* employable with young children. Yet I think that it remains an important question, and one which in earlier EYL eras has been more seriously treated, even if without any very conclusive results.

There is an interesting comparison to be drawn from past approaches to EYL courses. When the methodology was generally more uniform and not the focal point of interest, the area that was seen as the proper subject of discussion was the suitable linguistic content of language courses. Going back one step in time to L.G. Alexander's *Look, Listen and Learn!*, Teacher's Book One (1968) we find an inventory of some 506 lexical items carefully grouped under topic and grammatical headings, with an additional 80 or so formulaic/idiomatic phrases also classed by this author under vocabulary. This is a coursebook fully in the audio-lingual tradition, of which it is a commonplace to say that vocabulary often takes second place to the development of grammatical structures. However, *Look, Listen and Learn!* seems to have rather substantial vocabulary contents when seen in relation to the more 'lexically diluted' but educationally richer and methodologically more acquisition-orientated courses of the 1990s. All eight books, including *Look, Listen and Learn!*, seem to be comparable in the claims their authors make about intended period of use. The introduction to the Teacher's Book to *Look, Listen and Learn!* (page 6) gives an equation of 120 lessons at an expected 40 minutes each = 80 hours for a year's course, which is very similar in extent to the estimates given in the modern textbooks under review.

There is yet more interesting data about attitudes to vocabulary to be found in the YL movements of the earlier 1960s. I reproduce below a table provided in the chapter by W. F. Mackey, 'Trends and research in Methods and Materials' as his contribution to the volume *Languages and the Young School Child* (Stern (ed.), 1969). The figures given are the results of spot estimates given by participants at the 1966 Hamburg meeting of the UNESCO Institute for Education.

As Mackey remarks, this table is not entirely reliable, since it was based on guesstimates by national experts, and not based on careful counts of items in published coursebooks. As Mackey also says, 'in order to make such studies comparable it would be necessary to elaborate the standard units of measure-

Table 1 Estimated first-year active vocabularies (Mackey, 1969)

Country	Words	Hours	Length of lesson (mins)	Age	Average per hour
France	200	100			2
École Active Bilingue	300	60	20		5
Germany	600	200	45	10	3
Berlin experiment	150	80	20	8	2
Poland	350	100	45	11	3.5
Spain	250 400*	164	60	10–11	1.5–2.5
Ukraine	300	80	45		3
USSR	350	100	45		3.5
United Kingdom					
Nuffield experiment	250	95	30	10–14	2.5

* Depending on language

ment so that each term (like word and active) might have the same meaning for everyone.' This points to the same difficulties that I expressed above over the need to establish criteria for the modern analysis. The main point about Mackey's study for my purposes is, however, that it actually exists. As such it is one of many examples of serious interest in this earlier era in the issue of the quantity and nature of the words with which it is appropriate to build a language course.

Mackey's work also seems to reveal the same sort of 'teaching culture' difference in expectations about children's ability to cope with vocabulary that I have observed in the 1990s. When teachers from different countries are faced with information about the vocabulary contents of materials, the same 'facts' can be met with very different reactions by teachers from different countries even where approximately the same hours and facilities are available. These range from 'Is that all?' to 'Our children could never cope with that!'

Mackey goes on to make the point that 'in order for countries teaching foreign languages in primary schools to build their syllabuses, methods and materials on the actual language-learning capacities of children, much more information than we have at present is needed on the rate of foreign language acquisition.' That is, teachers' views of what is a suitable vocabulary target, could usefully be tempered by some hard research into what children in general actually can do, given optimum circumstances. The trail frustratingly peters out at this point, since I have found little evidence of such hoped-for research to refer to for the purposes of this paper. This to some extent makes the lack of professional consensus in the seven courses understandable. From the evidence of the teachers' books, it seems to be an issue that remains unexplored, or at least not addressed by any overt statements made by any of the authors.

Basis for choice of particular words

We have seen that there are wide differences in the bare number of words that are included in different courses, but so far there has been no discussion of the basis on which particular words might have been selected, and whether this tends to lead to overlap or a 'core' of words that one could expect to find in most courses.

To answer the question about overlap first, the contents of the seven word lists were looked at in detail. It was decided to concentrate on words at two opposite extremes:
1 Words that seemed to have at least a fair amount of common consent – words appearing in five, six, or seven out of seven courses were put in this category. A total of 113 words appeared in five or more books, but only 29 were found in all seven.
2 Words that were 'peculiar' to a single course.

More detailed results are given in Figure 2.

It can be seen that there is a rather low area of common consent, and that nearly half the words making up the total inventory of lexical items are unique to one or other of the books out of the seven. It might be hypothesised that

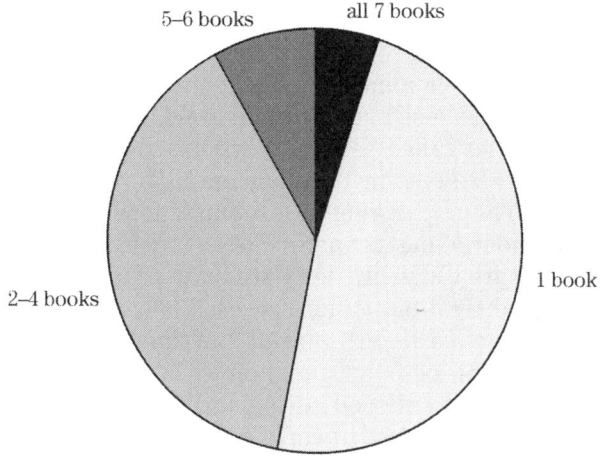

Figure 2 Distribution of vocabulary items

these 'unique presences' were most marked in those books with the largest total vocabulary, but this proved not to be the case. Unique presences were fairly evenly spread over the seven books. It should also be pointed out that the number of words present in five, six or seven of the books, low though it is, has been considerably inflated by the decision to keep in the numerals one to thirty as lexical items. The lists of the 'most popular' items are given in Appendix 2, and make interesting reading, for what they do not contain, as much as for what they do contain.

This variety and diversity tell us little about the principles on which the authors made their selection. A close look at the items on the vocabulary lists perhaps allows an interpretation that three common-sense procedures might have been used:
1 Studying the vocabulary implications of topics based on children's supposed centres of interest (e.g. pets and family).
2 Adding vocabulary that is useful for carrying out lessons in a school environment (e.g. blackboard, desk).
3 In books with a strong story line, introducing words which help to 'carry' the story, or give a character a special identity. It is here that the most striking differences between books may lie.

Data-driven means that could be used to inform vocabulary selection

It is interesting that in this age of enormous interest in corpus-based studies of natural language, no EYL course-designer to my knowledge has overtly based his or her work on a corpus of the language used by children who are native speakers of the target language. I say this, in the knowledge that, had this been the case, the publisher would certainly have seized upon this point and made it widely known to potential users.

It is notable on the other hand that in the 1960s, and even in the 1950s, researchers and materials designers took the issue of collecting and analysing data about real child language seriously, when teaching materials (foreign language courses, and also reading development materials for native speakers) were to be created. This is striking in circumstances in which facilities for recording data and undertaking its analysis were much less well developed and easy to use than they are today. An early study of young native speakers' oral language, to inform the creation of more accessible early reading development materials for native speakers, was that of Burroughs (1957), done without benefit of tape recorders, or much technology at all. Trainee teachers in a number of teacher-training colleges in England (specifically the Midlands of England) were assigned a project to carry out semi-structured conversations with two young pupils each (ages 5–6) and they were asked to 'record' (meaning 'write down', since there were no tape recording facilities available) each 'new' word used by a child. The results were collated and presented. The results were rough, since the lack of complete transcripts meant that no analysis of the different grammatical functions of words could be recovered. For example, a word such as 'turn' was listed only once, without information on whether it was used as a noun or a verb.

This study, crude though it was in some respects, nevertheless represented a real departure from previous approaches to syllabus design. Many of these earlier approaches looked not at what language real children could already use, but at 'what was required of them *a priori*' in already-existing reading materials. The dangers were pointed out by Burroughs as analysing not what children's oral language capacity was really like and then using it to create more accessible reading materials, but as analysing what some adult had decided they 'should' learn to read. There are warnings here for modern-day course-designers for EYL, who might well also work too far by adult intuition or by copying the efforts of previous writers through use of a syllabus based on the contents of existing textbooks.

The question could be raised whether books by future EYL writers could become more convergent in their vocabulary content, and a degree of fossilisation could be expected, because of the influence of increasingly available international tests and certificates aimed at Young Learners. For example, when the very influential Cambridge University UCLES Examination Board launched a set of Young Learners' Certificate examinations (1997), it published a syllabus largely expressed in terms of vocabulary. The syllabus has quite explicitly been announced as being drawn partly from an analysis of a number of named EYL textbooks, which are in turn listed as being suitable for preparation for these exams. It remains to be seen whether future published textbooks will adopt this consensus vocabulary as an *a priori* component of their language syllabuses, and it needs further serious consideration to see if this would be in any way justifiable.

In the 1960s carefully designed studies of native-speaking children's real language repertoire were carried out with the purpose of informing language-learning materials intended for the primary school level. In particular, the researchers and designers involved with the UK Nuffield French from Eight experiment, and the researchers at CREDIF (in the École Supérieure de Fontenay St Cloud, Paris) co-operated extensively to collect and analyse real child language data, organised around 'centres of interest' (topics in our terms), grammar and lexis. The results were shared for the development of French-teaching materials in the UK and for English-teaching materials in France. Leaving aside some historical changes in culture, interests, and therefore in vocabulary, the results do not look so very strange or un-usable today. The items most likely to change over time are the nouns, as different crazes, concepts and technological items come on to the scene. Summaries of this research, and the linguistic inventories arrived at, can be found in the chapters by Handscombe (on English) and by Leclerque (for French) in Stern (ed.) (1969).

The 1980s and 1990s saw a huge development of interest in corpus-based studies of authentic language use, promoted by the much greater technical resources for data gathering and analysis at our disposal. The way forward for EYL as well as for many other sectors of ELT may be in a balance between 'how to teach' and the carefully considered use of real language data provided by corpus analysis. The big 'general' seeming corpora, such as the Cobuild Corpus, based in Birmingham University, or the British National Corpus (BNC), based in Oxford University, reveal often unexpected information about how the English language is 'really used' in general. All instances of words have been tagged with code markings that will allow the teacher/materials-writer to investigate in detail different specific modes of language use (such as spoken versus written) or different specific domains of use (such as journalism versus academic articles on the same topic) and even to investigate language used by the two sexes and by age ranges. What, therefore, is on offer for course-designers for Young Learners of English?

There are many problems here, when course-designers seek corpus information on 'Young English'. There is nothing identifiable in the major general corpora that includes natural language use by very young native speakers as a category, although the Cobuild Corpus contains a number of texts taken from children's literature. My investigations revealed no very recent large-scale study of children's language that could directly provide input for designers of courses for the age-groups normally covered by EYL textbooks. A very interesting, slightly less recent study, however, is that by Raban (1988) covering oral language used by the age-group of 5–6. This was a re-working of the Bristol University oral data originally collected and analysed by Wells (1985) and it benefits from a 'tagging' for grammatical functions. This results in alphabetical, frequency and grammar category-based lists that enable the reader to discover aspects of native-speaking children's vocabulary not revealed by earlier studies such as that by Burroughs. Take, for example, the word 'like': a very popular word in EYL courses as a verb (there are many units on Likes and Dislikes) but the data reveals that it is used at least as often as a preposition, e.g. 'My cat is like a tiger' (my invented example). Only two of the textbooks under investigation included this use of the word. Course-designers of materials for children aged eight to eleven will need to think carefully about whether they feel that it is justifiable to use the model of younger children's use of language as a basis for their work for older age groups, but where the data reveals frequent types of expression that are not catered for in books for older learners, it is at least a signal to take stock of where we may be underproviding for their expressive needs. A modern corpus of children's language at the 'right' age is something to look forward to.

Even when such a corpus of children's language becomes available, we have to face an issue which concerns the reasons for which Young Learners are being taught English in most countries. When we design learning materials for older learners – teenage, young adult and adult learners – it is easier to envisage many of them wishing in a relatively short time to join the native speech or discourse community with which they most closely identify. Therefore, language knowledge developed from course materials based on appropriate corpus information will be highly relevant and pay high dividends for them. It is to be hoped that many more Young Learners will in coming years have the opportunity to 'join the discourse community' of their peers in other countries, for example through exchange visits or via pen-friends, and the ever increasing e-mail and Internet links. Corpus-based studies of 'Young Language' in these domains could be very valuable as information for future course-designers. However, for many Young Learners these opportunities will not be available soon enough for them still to be 'Young' when they take advantage of them. In most countries, the value of Young Learner teaching seems to be seen by school authorities as some sort of preparation for future study of the language at secondary level, whether it is to be seen in Giovanazzi's (1998) terms as a mere 'softening up' or as a serious building up of extensive language competence. It is not widely seen as something for 'here and now' or even 'tomorrow's' use outside the school situation. Corpora which allow study of aspects of genuine 'Young Language' may therefore probably not be seen as the major source of input for Young Learners' course material. The safe and tidy topic areas such as Colours and Pets could remain main foci for Young Learners' courses, while children speaking English as a native language will, like most children, not spend much real conversational time on these areas. They will continue to talk of more gritty issues such as friendship dynamics, rivalry, gossip and the latest fashion, and, of course, those very interesting and rude matters that tend not to find their way into course material. The closest to the rough and rude side of life many courses get is people 'feeling sick'. I have yet to meet a character actually 'being sick' somewhere embarrassing, or one of those lovable pets, that throng the coursebooks, 'doing a poo on the carpet'. Adult censorship will probably mean that this will never happen in coursebooks.

Choice based on linguistic criteria

There are linguistic criteria for vocabulary selection which, even in a teaching climate in which 'how not what' is the dominant interest, might repay consideration. Three important areas are the interaction of vocabulary with how grammar is treated, the ease with which the written form may be decoded by

Young Learners and the implications for pronunciation teaching. All of these may raise issues for how words are selected, sequenced and grouped.

Grammar

For an example of the first, I am indebted to my colleague Meriel Bloor (personal communication) for the insight that the verbs that are selected for primary-course inclusion often need more consideration for their grammatical behaviour. An instance of this from my data is the verb 'fly' used in two courses intransitively, and in another both intransitively and transitively, as in 'He is flying his kite'. Should course-designers try, in the examples they give, to clarify the scope of words like this, even though they may wish to avoid abstract grammatical analysis?

Spelling and decoding of written forms

A major issue concerns whether the phonological patterns of words in relation to their spelling should be taken more into account by EYL course-designers when they sequence and group the words that they identify as necessary or desirable for the course. Even though in countries such as Austria the Young Learners are deliberately kept away from English in its written form, in many more countries the written word is seen both as an object of learning in itself and as an instrument through which language is learned. It is perhaps worthwhile to consider the particular cases of teachers working in countries like Taiwan, Japan and Korea, where the writing system is different from the Roman alphabetic one and in which the dynamics between 'learning to read = decode English words' and using the words on the page as a support for English learning are very intense. In fact students from these countries following the Warwick MA in EYL have confirmed that traditions of English teaching often conform to parents' expectation that the very first lessons will include English graphemes, often given in alphabetical rather than the 'most phonically accessible' order. Even for learners in countries like Hungary or Italy, where the Roman alphabet is used, but whose own written code has a much more direct link with the phonemes of their language than is the case for English, the issue of deciding which words are to be seen on the page and in what groupings could benefit from some attention. In all the coursebooks under consideration, this could be seen as an issue, since at least a few words are seen printed on the page from the outset, although policies differ markedly over how much of the spoken language on the listening tapes is reproduced in printed form.

Applying a strong, traditionally phonics-based principle to vocabulary selection and ordering for an EYL coursebook, where words are seen on the page from the outset, would, of course, result in a ridiculously limited and artificial set of words for early lessons – a diet of 'bats', 'rats', 'cats' and 'mats' and a 'man with a van'. This is just the sort of problem that was for years identified as rendering the older and less well-designed controlled reading schemes for native speakers so unattractive and non-communicative. However, there is perhaps some sense in course-designers at least using their awareness of which English words can be easily sounded out from the more 'reliable' combinations of letters, so that Young Learners are not assailed at an early stage by a random exposure to written forms of words that are difficult to decode. They, after all, do not have the advantage that native-speaking children have of already knowing the language, and thus needing 'only' (!) to match written symbols with the sounds of familiar words.

Phonological considerations

It should also be borne in mind that, whether or not the YL are asked to cope with the relations between the written and spoken forms in any extensive way, the pronunciation of English presents some special difficulties in relation to many native languages. The large number of vowel phonemes (twenty in R.P.) compared with the restricted five or seven in many languages such as Italian or Spanish, the 'richness' of English when it comes to consonant clusters, and the much more variable position of stress-placement on syllables in lexical items compared with many languages are some cases in point (see Wells, 1994, for a discussion of these issues). Is there perhaps some value in bearing this in mind when deciding which words to focus upon first, next and later, and in seizing opportunities to create sets which have at least something in common in the phonological and spelling-to-sound areas?

A simple device, used in some courses but most consistently in Ashworth and Clark's very carefully planned *Stepping Stones*, is to make use of the names of characters to exemplify both particular phonemes and the more reliable letter

Look at the boy's /bɔɪɜ/ face /feɪs/.

This is his ....

These are his ....

eyes /aɪz/
nose /nəʊz/
mouth /maʊθ/
ears /ɪəz/
hair /heə/

Notes:
1 The remaining diphthong /ʊə/ is not covered, but this is agreed to be present in the speech of only some R.P. speakers, usually older and more conservative, and only in a few words, such as 'poor' /pʊə/.
2 The figure is not intended to represent a piece of material to be used directly with pupils, but rather to act as a reminder to teachers of the pronunciation opportunities present in this lexical set.

Figure 3 An attempt to bring together the eight diphthong phonemes of English within a lexical set – parts of the body

combinations. A recent insight of my own is that the pronunciation of most of the eight diphthongs of English can usefully be practised through items that are part of the lexical set of body parts, so popular in EYL textbooks (see Figure 3). This is an example of seizing an opportunity offered by words that have already been selected on other grounds, and there must be many more waiting to be discovered and built into the ways in which lexis is handled in Young Learners' courses.

What relationships of meaning are the children encouraged to explore through the lexis in EYL courses?

For space reasons, this section is briefer, and an indication only of areas in which more research needs to be done, and to which teachers need to pay particular attention. It is here that the 'what to teach' and the 'how to teach it' overlap in the strongest manner.

Many textbooks include activities that involve manipulating language in a rather mechanical way. Many seemingly 'grammar' activities are no more than an invitation to fill a slot with a clearly available vocabulary item with minimal grammar manipulation such as the selection of a singular or plural form. Many vocabulary activities involve little more than slot-filling within an obvious grammar context, or identifying and matching a word to a picture cue or other obvious context. Cameron (1994) points out the difficulties that this very limited view of both grammar and vocabulary poses for systematic language development in children, and goes on to point out, even more importantly, the need for materials and teachers to promote a view of 'words' that calls upon children's developing conceptual frameworks. Words need to be seen as fitting into hierarchies and oppositions in the semantic system of English, just as they do in the native language.

An analysis of the seven books discussed above seems to confirm Cameron's views, at least at the book-one level that has been the main focus of this article. Matching of words to pictures or to simple verbal contexts is predominant, and slot-filling – putting vocabulary items into gaps in sentences with minimal or no grammatical manipulation – is common. There is some element of building the networks and hierarchies of meaning that she refers to in some books where vocabulary items are to be sorted under headings, and children may potentially be guided to see that 'chicken' can come under 'Things to eat/Food' (as opposed to 'milk' which can come under 'Things to drink' – possibly a subset of 'Food'?), as well as being seen as a live creature and thus sorted under the appropriate heading in a list in which Animals and Birds are to be separated. It might further be asked if a chicken could ever be a sort of pet! The grammatical consequences of treating chicken as an edible substance (and thus a non-count noun) or as an individual entity (and thus a count noun) may be ones that the teacher or course-book writer chooses not to focus on, but both should be aware that the issue exists, as it does with cake, ice-cream, chocolate and many other things dear to children's stomachs.

In the majority of books, however, such lateral 'thinking around a word' does not take place, and even in those books where classification activities are used, vocabulary items tend to be seen as tokens to be identified, moved into fixed slots, but not often seen in their dynamics with other parts of the lexicon. Chickens are not often seen from so many angles, which seems a pity. Much of what Cameron draws our attention to as valuable in helping children build up hierarchical meaning networks demands the presence in a course of a number of superordinates under which to place lexical items. It might be expected that largely topic-based courses would have this built into the headings to lessons or units, such as the above-mentioned Animals, Pets and Food headings, but another rank of superordinates – 'vague mention' words that cover much of the real world, such as 'person', 'thing', 'place' – seem to be absent in most courses (see Appendix 3, page 70). This seems to be a pity, since so much can be done with rather simple language, using structures like 'a .... who/where/which ....' and the use of such language is at the basis of much of the circumlocution that strategic learners employ to get their meanings across when the precise word they need is not available.

This article has restricted itself to level one books (for eight-year-olds) in just seven series. The aim is to extend the study to cover more series. In addition, in order to give a fair assessment of what course writers are aiming at over the whole extent of their series, it will be necessary to shift the focus of the survey to trace whether there is any development of vocabulary policies in terms of acceleration in teaching/learning that can be traced in later books, and whether more complex operations involving lexical relationships are introduced through books two, three and upwards in the textbook series. A quick check with the next level up in the seven books under consideration does not suggest that this is a strong thread to be traced in most cases. Another important area that has not been touched on yet concerns the 'dosing' of words within the courses, the policies as to how many new words are introduced per lesson or unit and how these words are 'built in' to the rest of the course so as to have adequate opportunities for recycling.

Conclusion

All in all, the seven books analysed seem to be respectable attempts to do the impossible – that is to provide something that teachers in many different situations could take and use as a support for the most appropriate teaching possible. We all know that most teachers do more than this, and that their own efforts and experience of the children's interests and needs cover the gaps and remedy the deficiencies in the most minimal of textbooks. However, it seemed worthwhile to explore what could be said about the raw ingredients of some of the books that might be used in this way. Teachers who read this article might be encouraged to be more pro-active, to 'seize' the vocabulary ingredients in the courses that they may use, and seek new patterns of meaning within them, supplementing them and making sure that the book helps them to cover what their own students want and need to be able to do with English. Teachers who are meeting a book for the first time, deciding whether to use it or not, might be encouraged to look at what language it contains as well as how that language is practised and activated.

Appendix 1

Section of the spreadsheet printout showing the method of recording the presence or absence of each word in the seven books analysed

word	Book A	Book B	Book C	Book D	Book E	Book F	Book G	Total
animal	0	1	1	0	1	1	1	5
answer	1	1	0	0	0	0	0	2
any	1	0	0	0	0	0	0	1
apple	0	1	0	0	1	1	1	4
arm	1	0	1	1	1	1	1	6
armchair	0	0	0	0	1	0	0	1
around	1	1	0	0	0	0	0	2
artist	1	0	0	0	0	0	0	1
ask	1	1	0	0	0	0	0	2
at	1	1	0	0	0	0	1	3
at once	0	1	0	0	0	0	0	1

Notes:
It is convenient to use a spreadsheet for this type of work for a number of reasons. It is easy to insert a whole new row for each new word that is found in each book. If a word is present in a book, 1 is put into the appropriate cell in the spreadsheet. If it is not present, 0 is entered. The program allows the user to put in formulae such as an instruction to add up all the items in a row or in a column. Chart-drawing programs are also linked to the spreadsheet program so that results can be easily displayed in graph or other visual form.

Appendix 2a

Vocabulary items overlapping across books

Total range of vocabulary items found = 889
Items found in all seven books (= 29):
　　the numerals one to twelve
　　be, big, black, blue, book, brown, draw, green, in, nose, on, pencil, pink, red, sister, white, yellow

Items found in six out of seven books (= 43):
　　the numerals thirteen to twenty-one
　　arm, bag, bed, bird, brother, car, chair, dog, door, ear, eye, father, foot/feet, go, hair, hello, listen, long, mouse, mouth, name, number [n.], OK, orange, pen, rabbit, rubber, ruler, short, small, snake, stand up, table, television

Items found in five out of seven books (= 41):
　　animal, behind, boy, can [vb], cat, down, family, fat, fish, football, friend, girl, good, goodbye, grey, happy, have got, here, house, how many, ice-cream, look, of, open, please, purple, put, right, say, see, sit down, sock, square, stop, tall, taxi, toe, tooth/teeth, tree, window, write

Appendix 2b

The 'top twenty' words in frequency order within three grammatical categories taken from Raban (1988)

Nouns:
 Mummy, Mum, Ma, bit, Daddy, time, thing, way, Dad, man, things, house, baby, bed, boy, girl, door, water, dinner, minute

Adjectives:
 little, big, right, nice, good, dear, other, old, long, red, black, yellow, more, blue, funny, pink, silly, bigger, lovely, orange

Verbs (full verbs and modals only were counted on my word lists, so the list has been continued until a substantial number of these items have appeared):
 got, do, don't, is, have, can, going, want, look, go, get, know, come, are, put, be, see, can't, was, take, isn't, will, did, like, shall, haven't, won't, didn't, think, make, said, play, had, say, let, done, give

Appendix 3

Potential superordinate and 'vague mention' words found in the books

(The number of books in which each word is found is given in brackets):

animal	(5)
bird	(6)
clothes	(3)
colour	(5)
food	(2)
fruit	(2)
family	(5)
pet	(3)
toy	(3)
vegetable	(2)

'vague mention' words:
person	(0)
people	(2)
place	(0)
something	(3)
thing	(3)

Appendix 4

List of books analysed

Alexander, L.G., *Look, Listen and Learn! 1* Longman, 1968.
Ashworth, J. and Clark, J., *Stepping Stones 1* Collins, 1989.
Lobo, M.J. and Subira, P., *Big Red Bus 1* Heinemann, 1993.
McHugh, M. and Occhipinti, G., *Fanfare 1* Oxford University Press, 1993.
Revell, J. and Seligson, P., *Buzz 1* BBC English, 1993.
Rixon, S., *Tip Top 1* Macmillan, 1990.
Strange, D., *Chatterbox 1* Oxford University Press, 1989.
Vannuffel, P., Power, P., Palim, J. and Oxenden, C., *Crackerjack 1* Nelson, 1994.

6 'Natural Born Speakers of English': Code Switching in Pair- and Group-work in Hungarian Primary Classrooms

Marianne Nikolov
Janus Pannonius University, Pécs

P2: What's your name,...... seven. What's your name?
P1: I'm seven.
(Somlyódi and Vándor, 1995:6)

This paper looks at how Hungarian children interact in foreign language classrooms. Data collected in 111 observed classes are analysed to identify emerging patterns of peer–peer interaction. The paper discusses when, how, why and in what languages children exchanged information, applied for help and supported each other and compares the results to various educational contexts reviewed in the first part of this paper. It explores how willingness to interact in the target language is related to profiency, age and peer pressure.

Background to the research

The last decade has seen a shift of interest towards classrooms, and lessons have increasingly been perceived not only as pedagogic events, but also as social events (Prabhu, 1992). Classroom research on how interaction shapes second-language learning has so far 'contributed little to our understanding of how interaction affects acquisition' (Ellis, 1994:607), although work in pairs and small groups is widely seen as one of the essential features of communicative language teaching. Long and Porter (1985) argue that pair-work and group-work are useful as they increase language practice opportunities, improve the quality of student talk, help to individualise instruction, establish a positive affective climate, reduce anxiety and motivate learners to learn. Negotiation is also generally supposed to provide the kind of input and opportunities for output that promote second language acquisition (Pica, et al., 1996), though the benefits of small-group use of communicative activities '... may be more limited than had previously been assumed' (Pica and Doughty, 1985:132) even in second language contexts.

Studies on peer interaction in Young Learners' foreign language (FL) classrooms are hard to find, and most of the research comes from (1) second language/bilingual classrooms in the host environment where instruction is provided only in the target language; (2) immersion programmes where the school curriculum is fully or partly in the target language. These contexts vary not only in the amount and quality of input children are exposed to, but also in the extent to which learners, or learners and teachers, share a mother tongue.

In this section I will try to provide a short overview of what has been found so far concerning child–child interaction in second language, immersion and foreign language classrooms.

Wong-Fillmore (1985; 1991:52) identified three components necessary for children to acquire a second language in the host environment:

1 Learners who realise that they need to learn the target language and are motivated to do so.
2 Speakers of the target language who know it well enough to provide learners with the input and the help they need for learning it.
3 A social setting which brings learners and target-language speakers into frequent enough contact to make second language acquisition (SLA) possible.

Wong-Fillmore found that in a second language learning context children who scored high in measures of sociability and communicative need were generally good learners, but only in social settings where they were outnumbered by speakers of the target language, and where they could interact freely with one another.

In foreign language learning (FLL) contexts the situation is different, and the components need to be modified in the following way:

1 Young Learners who do not need the language and do not realise that they may need it in the future but are open to new experiences in general, and whose parents may be motivated for the child to learn the target language.
2 Teachers who know it well enough to provide the learners with access to the language and the help they need for learning it.
3 A classroom setting within the social setting which brings learners and teachers/peers into frequent enough contact to make FLL possible (Nikolov, 1994:57-62).

Second language classrooms

Pease-Alvarez and Winsler (1994) used a combined ethnographic quantitative perspective based on extensive field observations and interviews in a fourth-grade classroom containing Spanish-speaking learners of English as a second language. It was found that, although as these children progressed through the grade their use of their native language at school tended to decrease in the English-only milieu, they nevertheless 'used considerable amounts of Spanish when conversing about non-academic topics and when participating in small-group instructional events' (Pease-Alvarez and Winsler, 1994:530). This was in spite of the teacher's reliance on English only. Interestingly, the majority of the children spoke to themselves in English, and code-switched very little in their private speech while working on cognitive tasks, but 15 per cent of the children's speech with their teacher contained some Spanish. The following language pattern variation was found as a function of activity: 'on task' discussions on academic tasks were usually first in English, then children chatted with a classmate in Spanish about an unrelated topic ('off task'), and then returned to the task, usually in English again.

Immersion programmes

As far as immersion programmes are concerned, one of the most persistent problems identified by Tarone and Swain (1995) in Canadian immersion programmes is that pupils tend to use the target language more frequently when they are younger than they do in later years of learning. In their view, a sociolinguistic perspective is needed to examine classrooms where diglossia is the norm. The second language is the superordinate or formal language variety, and the native language is reserved for use in informal social interactions as the vernacular language style. They argue that even though using the target language is cognitively harder than using the mother tongue, younger immersion children use the target language more frequently than later on during their studies, and they tend to use it for academic topics and the first language for social interactions. They suspect that the academic language of the immersion programmes prevents children from getting enough input in the vernacular style, although even children in two-way immersion classrooms tend to rely on the majority language vernacular in peer–peer interactions. They hypothesise that 'pre-adolescents and adolescents need a vernacular style as a way of signalling their identities' (1995:160), and, since the only complete vernacular language at children's disposal is the native language vernacular, they rely on it. By the fifth and sixth grades, they prefer using the native language in peer–peer social discourse, and the target language becomes the institutional language of academic discourse.

Foreign language contexts

Most of the available studies in this area concern older learners. For example, Poulisse and Bongaerts (1994) investigated unintentional first-language use in three groups of Dutch learners of English. They involved university students (age 19–22) after eight years of English study, 15–16 year-old students after five years of studying English, and 13–14 year-olds after three years of English instruction. Poulisse and Bongaerts found that the use of L1 words during L2 production was frequent and proficiency-related, with more use of L1 by the less proficient students. According to their explanation, reduced automaticity of speech production may have played a role in the case of beginners. This finding is in contrast with the immersion classroom observation according to which adolescents with higher proficiency tend to switch back to L1 more frequently than younger and less proficient learners.

In my own classrooms even the most motivated adults at the advanced level – those in methodology seminars with pre- and in-service students and teachers of EFL – typically switch to Hungarian in pair- and group-work, except for the pair nearest to the tutor. When participants share the mother tongue, it seems simply unnatural to talk the target language for managing a task, setting the scene, discussing details. Further empirical research is necessary to reveal patterns in adult peer–peer interaction in foreign classrooms.

As far as children in the foreign language context are concerned, Nikolov

(1994:161-167) describes how Young Learners between the ages of six and fourteen gradually begin to use the target language creatively for their own interpersonal communicative purposes and considers changes in the role of the teacher as a model. Young learners follow the teacher as a model without any criticism: even when she makes mistakes they will not want to accept that the teacher may be wrong. Children around puberty gradually realise that the target language represents institutional discourse and voluntary users are often labelled as trying to please the teacher. This is one of the reasons why children around the ages of 11 to 14 tend to use less English and switch back to Hungarian in spite of their good command of the target language. By using the mother tongue they indicate to one another that belonging to the peer group is more important than behaving according to a classroom norm that reflects the authority of the teacher. The fact that children do not code-switch in writing is one of the arguments supporting this claim: when submitting a written paper to the teacher, peers are not part of the audience, whereas in oral contributions children are anxious not to be judged by the others. This is the reason why some of the children in my own classes from the age of 11 to 12 did not want to perform any role-play before the rest of the class and wanted to choose their audience. Even in an ideal situation when the same teacher taught the learners for the full length of their eight-year study, when a peer, after a short stay in Britain, represented an authentic vernacular model of the target language (using 'yeah' instead of the teacher's 'yes'), children started following the peer model and wondered if the teacher should not do the same to avoid losing face (Nikolov, 1994:173-174).

According to Chaudron (1988:109), studies on interaction between learners reveal no clear trends in differences between classroom organisational structures, but the critical factor appears to be the language task. Most probably the task is one of the crucial factors in determining how learners interact, but the status of the first and the target languages is also very important.

The present study
The present study is an attempt to evaluate to what extent the findings of the above-mentioned studies are relevant to the case of Hungarian pupils learning English as a foreign language.

Participants and data collection
Data were collected during the 1995–97 academic years by trained, pre-service English majors of Janus Pannonius University who wrote seminar papers on their projects. Altogether 111 classes were tape-recorded in 37 randomly chosen groups all over Hungary. Children's interactions during pair- and group-work were transcribed and analysed. Each group was observed and taped three times.

Table 1 illustrates the distribution of data collection across school grades and age groups. It was impossible to observe an equal number of classes in each grade, thus very young (6–7 year-olds) and older children (12–14 year-olds) were less frequently tape-recorded than the age groups in between.

Table 1 Distribution of number of groups and observed classes across grades and age groups

Grade and age of children	1st 6–7	2nd 7–8	3rd 8–9	4th 9–10	5th 10–11	6th 11–12	7th 12–13	8th 13–14
Number of groups observed	2	2	7	7	9	4	2	4
Number of observed classes	6	6	21	21	27	12	6	12

Hypotheses

It was hoped that – in spite of the observer's paradox – pupils would provide valuable empirical data on how they interacted with one another in foreign language classes. I hypothesised that in controlled tasks they would use the target language more frequently, whereas in less controlled circumstances they would rely more on the mother tongue. I also hoped to find out how peer interaction changed with age and the development of proficiency. It was also hypothesised that some teachers would be more successful at scaffolding children's learning and examples of 'good practice' would be found in the data. The inquiry into children's learning was meant to represent qualitative rather than quantitative research design in the non-participant ethnographic tradition.

Patterns of interaction in Hungarian FL classrooms

In all 111 classes children were enthusiastic, motivated to participate and well behaved. They all seemed to be interested in what was required from them, and also in the observers' aims and the equipment used for tape-recording their talk, but the latter focus soon lost its novelty value and children seemed to behave naturally.

Irrespective of age, level and task, whenever children were expected to work in pairs or small groups they typically switched back to Hungarian and used the first language more frequently than English. The pupil–pupil talk recorded and transcribed was rarely overheard by the teacher, so observers were able to get useful insights into how children interacted when the teacher was not around. On the whole, more first language talk or silence characterised the observed children than talk in the target language either in controlled teacher-fronted activities or during individual or pair-work. The teacher's use of the target language did not influence the extensive use of the mother tongue in pair-work across all age groups, although some useful examples have been found where teachers scaffolded children's learning successfully by integrating pupils' mother-tongue talk into their target language discourse. On the other hand, older learners tended to use the target language more frequently in cases where the teacher refused to use Hungarian but was prepared to provide help in the target language having understood pupils' Hungarian talk.

In my analysis I will focus on the pupil–pupil interactions observed in the 37 different groups. Further analysis will be necessary to clarify the roles played by teachers' talk and teacher-pupil interaction.

The following patterns emerged:

Generally, in controlled practice children gave the required answers or repeated after the teacher without interacting with one another. Consequently in these cases more target language was used than in less controlled tasks. How much of the rote-learned texts repeated by the children was understood and represented comprehensible input to peers is a question to explore in further research.

In these classrooms children were 'disciplined', did not initiate conversations and tended to work quietly and individually, relying on the safe pattern of the IRF (teacher initiation – learner response – teacher follow-up) cycle so typical of the institutional discourse type (Seedhouse, 1996) of classroom communication.

When pupils said something, these examples fell into the two wide student talk categories according to the Flanders' Interaction Analysis Categories (FLINT):
a) Student talk – response initiated by the teacher.
b) Student talk – initiation reflecting students' own ideas (Allwright, 1988:60).

Most of the children's discourse can be characterised as 'on task,' whereas 'off task' talk was very rare in our data. Children in the lower grades did not use cumulative or exploratory talk even in Hungarian, as no such opportunities were provided in the tasks. On the other hand, 13–14 year-olds did provide examples of cumulative as well as exploratory talk in the target language when they negotiated meanings, supported each other's learning, or wanted to show off to one another.

The above wide categories relate interaction to classroom tasks, and the data can be further classified as below (see Appendix for transcription conventions following van Lier, 1988).

Pupil asks peer for help and/or clarification

The examples in this category include only on-task talk; the aim of discourse is to come up to the teacher's expectations by fulfilling the task without asking the teacher for help, as it can be provided by a peer as well.

EXTRACT 1 (CLASS OF 7–8 YEAR-OLDS READING ALOUD)

    1 T: Péter, read on.
    2 P1: Hol tartunk most? (Where are we?) ((P1 turning to neighbour))
    3 P2: Itt. (Here.) ((points to paragraph))
    4 P1: ((reads on))
(Fóti, 1995:7)

EXTRACT 2 (13–14 YEAR-OLDS IN WHOLE-CLASS ACTIVITY)

    1 T: Let's have some ideas about newspapers.
    2 P1: ((whispering to P2)) Hol van a könyvben? (Where is it in the book?)

3 P2: A hatvanadik oldalon. (On page sixty.)
4 T: May I ask you not to open your books?
(Pék, 1996:11)

In extracts 1 and 2 Pupil 1 applied for help in a teacher-fronted activity, as P1 was not paying attention and wanted to avoid trouble. In extract 1 P1 would not be expected to be able to ask for help in the target language, whereas in extract 2 he should have been able to do so in English but did not. In both examples P1 got the required answer in Hungarian quickly. Similar exchanges were frequent but rarely mutual: it was usually the same pupil applying for help. Fortunately, only one example of refusal was found in the data (extract 5) indicating that children tended to be supportive to one another.

EXTRACT 3 (9–10 YEAR-OLDS IN PAIR-WORK)

1 P1: Hogy van az, hogy nincs? (How do you say I don't have?)
2 P2: I have no pet.
3 P1: I have no pet.
(Kovács, 1995:3)

EXTRACT 4 (9–10 YEAR-OLDS IN GROUP-WORK)

1 P1: Cat az kutya? (Does cat mean dog?)
2 P2: ((nods))
(Kovács, 1995:3)

Extracts 3 and 4 illustrate how children apply for help in pair-work when one of them (P2) is supposed by a peer (P1) to know more English and to be willing to help. P2's answers supported this expectation, though in extract 3 not only was the requested help given, but P2 gave an expansion – the full correct answer to the controlled task – while P1 was trying to come to the right solution by piecing it together from two analysed components while thinking in Hungarian. In extract 4 it seems that P2 was not listening to the question.

Below is the only example of a peer refusing to help:

EXTRACT 5 (8–9 YEAR-OLDS FILLING IN GAPS)

1 T: Now you have to fill in the gaps, fill in with the missing body parts.
2 P1: Ezt nem értem mit kell csinálni. (I don't understand what to do.) ((whispering to P2))
3 P2: ((working in notebook)) Hagyjál már békén, ne lökdöss már! (Leave me alone, stop pushing!)
(Merza, 1997:3)

Here P2 did not want to share the instruction in Hungarian, although the teacher was quite tolerant of peer interaction. Finally, P1 did not ask anyone else but simply copied what P2 was doing.

Pupils instruct and discipline each other

The vast majority of examples here come from on-task pupil–pupil talk, except for the following two examples in which P1's comment is not related to a task but to classroom norm:

EXTRACT 6 (6–7 YEAR-OLD GIRL TELLING OFF A BOY)

> P1: Szép a cipőd, csak nem a széken! (Your shoes are nice but not on the chair.)
> P2: ((takes feet off the chair))
> (Kutas, 1997:5)

EXTRACT 7 (10–11 YEAR-OLD GIRLS IN READING ACTIVITY)

> 1 P1: Olvasd már! (Read it!)
> 2 P2: Jó. Tiszta kócos vagy. (Okay. Your hair is all untidy.)
> 3 P1: Kezdd már el! (Start reading!)
> (Tavali, 1996:7)

While in extract 6 P2 behaved as requested, in extract 7 P2's comment was considered irrelevant, and P1 focused back on the reading task, thus forcing P2 to act as required.

In the following extracts children of various ages echo the teacher's expectations by wording their instructions in a peculiar way in Hungarian. In the taped sessions teachers did not use the same expressions in Hungarian but it is possible that in other classes they did. All the examples in this category were related to the management aspect of the tasks, thus children were fulfilling one of the roles of the teacher.

EXTRACT 8 (CLASS OF 6–7 YEAR-OLDS IS VERY NOISY IN A GUESSING GAME)

> 1 P1: D-O-G ((spelling word to be guessed))
> 2 P2: Dog!
> 3 T: Is it a dog?
> 4 P1: Igen. (Yes.)
> 5 T: Right.
> 6 P3: Yes, nem igen. Angolul kell beszélni. (Yes, not igen. You must speak English.)
> (Somlyódi and Vándor, 1995:4)

EXTRACT 9 (CLASS OF 6–7 YEAR-OLDS GUESSING AN ANIMAL IN A COVERED PICTURE)

> 1 P1: Is it a fish?
> 2 P2: No, it isn't. Aki nyavalyog, azt nem választom. (I will not choose the ones who whine.)
> 3 P3: Lécci... (Please...)
> (Somlyódi and Vándor, 1995:9)

While in extract 8 the register in Hungarian could be that of a teacher, in extract 9 the vernacular style of P2 (turn 2) is answered in the same style by P3 which would not be acceptable with a teacher. Although it is also possible that children were repeating the teacher's language this expression was not heard during the observation. In addition, extract 8 reflects children's desire to speak the target language and they warn one another to do so, whereas in later years they tend to use the mother tongue. In extract 8 children are absolute beginners and yet they still wish to speak English and try to persuade one another to do so. Obviously, some of the children as early as at the age of six to seven realise that speaking English represents institutional discourse, and having to speak it in class, is one of the rules.

EXTRACT 10 (9–10 YEAR-OLDS READING IN PAIRS)

    1 P1: Ezt olvasd el, ami előtte van. (Read what's before it.)
    2 P2: ((not reading))
    3 P1: Na, Mátéka, te kezdesz. (Well, Mátéka, you begin.) Come on.
    (Györök, 1996:6)

In this extract P1 first told P2 what to do and, when he did not do it, P1 asked him to start reading by using his name (Máté), adding an unusual diminutive suffix, reflecting perhaps patronizing or friendship, and added in the target language 'Come on' as an encouragement, or perhaps using the teacher's expression, knowing that he would be able to understand it.

In the following examples children start out negotiating in Hungarian how to manage the task, and then shift both focus and style to discuss the content as real communication in the two languages.

EXTRACT 11 (10–11 YEAR-OLDS IN CONTROLLED PAIR-WORK)

    1 P1: Jó, akkor kérdezz. (Okay, you ask.)
    2 P2: Te kérdezz. (You ask.)
    3 P1: Na jó. (Okay.) How long do snake live?
    4 P2: Snakes live..... várjál csak (wait)..... 80 years. Most te kérdezd tőlem a rinocéroszt. Nem, inkább kérdezd a pacit. (Now you ask me the rhinoceros. No, you'd rather ask the horsie.)
    5 P1: How long do horses live?
    (Mózes, 1995:9)

After deciding in turns 1 to 3 whose turn it was, P2 was trying to focus on horses by suggesting to P1 what to ask. The negotiation went on in the mother tongue with a child-language vocabulary item 'paci' used for horse, indicating a special interest in this animal, whereas the dialogue to be practised continued in English representing the academic on-task language, where 'horse' was used as an equivalent. This may be an example supporting the claim made by Tarone and Swain (1995) that children code-switch when they lack the necessary language. On the other hand, after negotiating the choice of animal, the children switched back to English.

EXTRACT 12 (10–11 YEAR-OLDS IN GUESSING GAME)

    1 P1: Are you afraid of bees?
    2 P2: ......
    3 P1: Mondd már meg, hogy miért félsz! (Say why you are afraid!)
    4 P2: Miért? Mert megcsíp. (Why? Because it stings.) Sting.
    5 P1: Are you afraid of snakes?
    6 P2: Yes, I am.
    7 P1: Gondoltam. Igen..... (I thought so....) and why?
    8 P2: Why, why? Sharp teeth.
    (Tóth, 1995:9)

Here again children first focused on the prescribed task in English and, when P2 got stuck, P1 tried to give an instruction and paraphrased the English question in Hungarian. P2, as if prompted, asked back and gave an answer in the mother tongue and then the verb required in the target language. P1's turn 5 indicated acceptance of the answer and the rote-learnt dialogue went on. In turn 7 P1 again commented on the truth value of the answer and continued the conversation. P2's answer focused on the reason, representing genuine communication.

In these stretches of discourse children seem to distinguish between the uses of the two languages in the same way as learners in immersion programmes and bilingual classes, as they use the vernacular style represented by Hungarian for interpersonal communication, and the target language for the academic task. English is rarely integrated into their social language use.

Sometimes the content of the question is so challenging that children start a private conversation on the topic in Hungarian:

EXTRACT 13 (8–9 YEAR-OLDS IN TEACHER-CONTROLLED DIALOGUE)

>   1 T: Do you like .... coffee?
>   2 P1: ((to P2)) Attól függ, milyen kávé. (Depends on what coffee.)
>   3 P2: ((to P1)) Én mindent szeretek. (I like everything.)
>   (Mándy, 1996:7)

An unusual comment was taped in a first-grade class. Private tutoring is quite frequent in secondary schools, and it seems that some parents also hire private teachers as soon as their child starts primary school. Children were practising new vocabulary items, and the pupil addressed had previously boasted of knowing it all from a private teacher called Annamária. The reference to the private tutor is definitely sarcastic, and the learner used Hungarian vernacular style as it was unavailable in English.

EXTRACT 14 (7 YEAR-OLD REPROACHING A PEER)

>   L: Látod, hiába tanultad te már azt az Annamária nénidnél, mi is tudjuk! (You see, you learnt it in vain with your Aunt Annamária, we also know it.)
>   (Mándy, 1996:7)

Pupil provides support by giving explanation
While only extract 14 represented serious criticism towards a peer in our data and just one request was turned down (extract 5), being helpful and supporting one another was typical among the children.

EXTRACT 15 (CLASS OF 6–7 YEAR-OLDS ABOUT TO SING A SONG)

>   1 T: Girls be quiet, just the boys!
>   2 Girl 1: Csak a lányok? (Only girls?)
>   3 T: ((nodding)) Attila, why don't you sing it?
>   4 Girl 1: Te fiú vagy. (You are a boy.)
>   5 T: Aren't you a boy?
>   6 Boy 1: Én nem énekelek. (I am not singing.)
>   7 Girl 2: Kiesett a foga. (He has lost his tooth.)
>   8 Boy 2: Lány vagy? (Are you a girl?)
>   9 Boy 1: Nem. Én énekeltem. (No. I was singing.)

10 T: No, you haven't sung!
(Somlyódi and Vándor, 1995:5)

In turn 4 Girl 1 was trying to be helpful presupposing that Boy 1 (Attila) would now understand the instruction of the teacher. Girl 2 had more insight into Boy 1's difficulties and implied that without front teeth he was not able to sing. Boy 2 wanted to tease him and got a negative reply. In turn 9 Boy 1 answered 'no' in reply to turn 8 and before replying to turn 3. Obviously, he was more sensitive to peer criticism than to the teacher's comment.

EXTRACT 16 (CLASS OF 9–10 YEAR-OLDS SINGING)

1 P1: De mindenkinek kell énekelni. (But all must sing.)
2 P2: De én nem tudok. (But I can't.)
3 P1: De tudsz. Egyszerű. Meg kell próbálni. (But you can. It's simple. You must try.)
4 P2: ((starts singing quietly with the others))
(Darázs, 1997: 4)

In this example P2 was not singing with the others, so P1 first acted as a teacher, then provided support and succeeded in persuading P2.

EXTRACT 17 (CLASS OF 6–7 YEAR-OLDS COLOURING AND WRITING)

1 T: What colour is this?
2 PP: Orange.
3 P1: Ide kell írni, hogy orange. (You have to write orange here.) ((pointing to workbook page of P3))
4 P2: Nem írni kell, hanem rajzolni. (You don't have to write it but draw it.) ((leaning over to P3))
5 P3: Ide a szivárvány mellé? (Here beside the rainbow?)
6 P2: ((demonstrates what to do and P3 does so))
(Somlyódi and Vándor, 1995:8)

In extract 17 three children interacted as P2 overheard P1's discussion with P3. As the teacher did not tolerate a lot of Hungarian, P2 finally demonstrated the activity.

EXTRACT 18 (6–7 YEAR-OLD GIRLS PRACTISING PRESCRIBED DIALOGUE)

1 P1: Hello.
2 P2: Hello.
3 P1: I'm Alexandra.
4 P2: I'm Orsi.
5 P1: What's your name?
6 P2: What's your name?
7 P1: Én kérdezem tőled, hány éves vagy. (I'm asking you how old you are.)
8 P2: What's your name,..... seven. What's your name?
9 P1: I'm seven.
10 P2: Hello.
11 P1: Hello.
12 P2: Goodbye.

13 P1: Goodbye.
(Somlyódi and Vándor, 1995:6)

Extract 18 illustrates how children try to come up to expectations. They had practised the rote-learnt dialogue as a whole-class activity, and now they were supposed to act it out in pairs. They memorised unanalysed chunks of the target language and knew some of the meanings of what they were saying. In turn 7 P1 wanted to help by translating for P2, but they still did not get the question right. Note, that in Hungarian 'Hello' may be used both when meeting and when leaving someone. Thus, in turns 10 and 11 the girls said goodbye in Hungarian, and then in English.

EXTRACT 19 (CLASS OF 6–7 YEAR-OLDS AFTER LOOKING AT PICTURE BOOKS)

1 T: Shut your books. Shut your books.
2 P1: Csukd be a könyved. (Shut your book.)
3 T: Shut it.
4 P1: Csukd be! (Shut it!) ((exchange repeated two more times))
5 T: People, shut the book. Àgnes, shut your book!
6 PP: Àgi, csukd be a könyved!! (Àgi, shut your book!!)
(Somlyódi and Vándor, 1995:6)

In this example first only one child tried to help Àgi by translating the teacher's instructions word for word. In turn 6 several students shouted out the same instruction, and she shut her book. Neither the teacher, nor the children mimed the activity.

EXTRACT 20 (10–11 YEAR-OLD GIRLS PREPARING FOR PAIR-WORK)

1 T: Okay, Janka, would you like to be a shop assistant?
2 P1: ((whispering to P2)) Eladó? (Shop assistant?)
3 P2: ((whispering to P1)) Aha, akarsz eladó lenni? (Yes, would you like to be a shop assistant?)
4 P1: No.
(Somogyi and Baksa, 1995:9)

Similarly to extract 19, a peer translated for P1 but only after she applied for help. Although P1 only wanted to check a single vocabulary item (shop assistant), P2 confirmed the question and translated the whole of turn 1 of the teacher, using unnecessary expansion similarly to extract 3. In turn 4 pupil 1 switched back to English.

EXTRACT 21 (10–11 YEAR-OLD GIRLS IN A GUESSING GAME)

1 P1: Has it got long neck?
2 P2: Yes, it has.
3 P1: Bird?
4 P2: Yes.
5 P1: Has it got a ... hosszú vagy rövid a csőre? (Is its beak long or short?)
6 P2: Rövid. (Short.)
7 P1: Akkor ostrich. (Then it is an ostrich.)
(Tóth, 1995:8)

A similar cycle can be identified in extract 21, but here peers were working in pairs without the teacher overseeing them. In turn 5 P1 switched to Hungarian to bridge a gap. Also, P1 combined two questions and in turn 7 gave the name of the bird from the limited choice learnt in English, introduced by a Hungarian word. They said what they could in the target language, and what was beyond them in the mother tongue. They creatively integrated their background knowledge of biology although the words were unknown to them in English.

Pupils correct one another

Sometimes children corrected one another both in teacher-fronted activities and in pair- or group-work. In the observed classes only a few examples of peer correction were found. The majority of teachers corrected all the errors on the spot and did not invite children to do so. Other teachers ignored errors, paraphrased for pupils and corrected them selectively. On the whole, young children did not seem to be sensitive to each other's errors and rarely noticed them. As will be seen in the examples of 13–14 year-olds, children become both more critical and more sensitive in later years.

EXTRACT 22 (CLASS OF 6–7 YEAR-OLDS FOCUSING ON SPELLING)

    1 T: Let's find, let's find words...
    2 P1: Yeah...
    3 T: er::... with 'v', 'v'.
    4 P2: villa (fork)
    5 P3: Ez nem jó. (It is no good.)
    (Somlyódi and Vándor, 1995:9)

In extract 22 P3 spontanously replied to P2 as the answer was in Hungarian but the teacher did not take any notice.

EXTRACT 23 (9–10 YEAR-OLDS IN CONTROLLED PRACTICE IN PAIRS)

    1 P1: I have breakfast at half past three.
    2 P2: Nem ebéd? (Not lunch?) ((following English syntax))
    (Horváth, 1997:14)

Children practised a rote-learned dialogue in extract 23. Although P2 asked back in the mother tongue, turn 2 follows the syntactic rules of the target language as a verbal suffix is missing (Nem ebédelsz?).

Students manage task

Hungarian was exclusively used for task management purposes. Some of the examples are quite short, others are lengthy.

EXTRACT 24 (10–11 YEAR-OLD GIRLS CHANGING ROLES)

    1 P1: Which wine would you like sir?
    2 P2: A bottle of red wine.
    3 P1: Most megint csere. (Now change again.) I'd like the menu please.
    (Horváth, 1997:5)

Extract 25 (three 9–10 year-old boys discussing role-play task)

    1 P1: Na, én leszek a Mutt. (Well, I'll be Mutt.)
    2 P2: Ki lesz a rádiós? (Who will be the reporter?)
    3 P3: Én leszek a rádiós. Én leszek a rádiós meg a... (I will be the reporter. I will be the reporter and the...)
    4 P2: Én leszek a rádiós meg az apa. (I will be the reporter and the father.)
    5 P3: Én leszek a rádiós meg a Mutt. (I will be the reporter and Mutt.)
    6 P1: Akkor figyelj. Te vagy az apa meg a rádiós. Nem, a Bence a rádiós, te meg az apa meg Mutt. (Then listen. You are the father and the reporter. No, Bence is the reporter and you are the father and Mutt.)
    7 P3: Én vagyok a Mutt. (I am Mutt.)
    8 P1: Csönd! Ne... (Quiet! Don't..)
    9 P3: Jól van. (Okay.)
    10 P2: Na... Animal pictures, free in packets. ((they start acting out the prescribed role-play))
    (Görbicz, 1996:16)

In spite of the difference in length, extracts 24 and 25 show the same pattern: negotiation on task management always happened in Hungarian, while the task itself was performed in the required target language. As can be seen in extract 24, children are aware of the institutional features of their discourse: they are doing a restaurant activity to practise language and they swap roles using Hungarian, as this is not part of the task.

Extract 25 does not represent an extremely long stretch of classroom discourse as in several cases children spent even more time staking out roles and managing tasks in Hungarian than actually implementing them in the target language. In the above example only one turn was in English out of 10. Also, it is important to note that the language necessary for this particular negotiation would have been at the children's disposal but it never occurred to them to talk in English.

In my view, this is the turning point in children's use of the target language. Speaking English means using the language of the institutional context represented by the teacher. Around puberty children start identifying with peers rather than teachers and that is the reason why they tend to use the target language less and less. Learners volunteering an answer in English in my own classes in the seventh and eighth grades were often perceived by peers as trying to be teacher's pets and children regularly commented by saying: 'Kis pedál, azt hiszed más nem tudja?' 'Kis okos, puncsos.' (You swat, you think others don't know it? How smart, clinger/pleaser.)

The last example represents the oldest age group in our data base. In extract 26 eighth-graders were preparing a role-play using conditionals.

Extract 26 (13–14 year-old boys preparing a role-play)

    1 P1: If you....
    2 P2: Mit nézel arra, én a Drávavölgyivel vagyok. (Why are you looking there, I am with Drávavölgyi.)
    3 P3: Én meg a vizilovakkal. (And I'm with the hippos.) ((laughs))
    4 P1: I will cut your grass.

5 P2: Mi? (What?) ((laughs)) What?... You stupid.
6 P1: If you wouldn't go from my field with your machines.... I will..
7 P2: Micsoda? (What?)
8 P1: Ha nem viszed te... el a gépekkel... (If you don't take it away.... with the machines...)
9 P2: Jó, értem, én azt értem, csak azt nem értem... (Okay, I understand, I do, I just don't understand...)
10 P1: Err::..... I will damage your car.
11 P2: If you damage ..... my car nincs is autóm (I don't even have a car.) ((laughs))
12 P1: Nem baj, akkor is megrongálom. (It doesn't matter, I will damage it anyway.)
13 P2: If you damage my car.... I will... burn your house. ((laughs))
14 P1: If you burn my house .... ((laughs)) I will kill you. ((laughs))
15 P2: If you kill me... ((laughs))
16 P1: Akkor te már megdöglöttél (Then you have kicked the bucket.) ((laughs))
17 P2: Then I call the police. ((laughs))
18 P1: If you call the police ... er::.... I will tell them ... you broke my arm.
19 P2: (unintelligible)
20 P1: Nem értem ám mer makogsz. (I don't understand 'cause you're stuttering.)
21 P2: Akkor sakkozzunk. (Then let's play chess.)
22 P1: Okay, play chess. Készen vagyunk Gabi néni. (We are ready Miss Gabi.)
23 P2: A ló kezd, hat lépésben mattot ad a királynőnek. (The Knight starts and checkmates the Queen in six moves.)
24 T: Are you ready?
25 PP: Yes, yes.
(Kusz, 1997:14)

P1 and P2 kept challenging each other, both in Hungarian and in English. Obviously, their language competence would have allowed them to use English only, but they kept switching codes. Turn 3 refers to the title of a film using the same pattern as the second part of turn 2. In turn 7 P2 seemed to apply for help and when P1 translated for him in turn 8 (the translation is not grammatical in Hungarian), he refused to accept it, so P1 went on in English. The discourse carried on on two levels: one representing the language task spiced with code switching, and the other representing the competition between the two boys. They were both consciously breaking classroom norms by using Hungarian, and finally decided to give up the task and started playing chess in Hungarian. P2 indicated the end of the formal task by suggesting in Hungarian that they should play chess in turn 21, to which P1 replied in turn 22 in English, then indicated to the teacher in Hungarian that they were finished with the role-play.

Conclusions

It is hard to tell how much the observers' presence influenced classroom processes. In some cases children were obviously not used to pair- or group-work and their teachers devoted minimal time to them, while in other groups learners interacted with one another with ease, as part of their routine. Also, classrooms differed in the amount of Hungarian tolerated: in teacher-fronted activities, in some cases no interaction took place at all and several children did not say a word.

On the whole, interaction and the amount of input in English were on a surprisingly low level, and I have doubts as to how much of the latter was comprehensible to all the learners. This may be one of the reasons why some teachers did not use pair-work in their classes. Further research is necessary to find out how interaction, the amount of input in the target language and success in FLL are interrelated.

The teacher's use of the target language did not seem to influence how much the children relied on the mother tongue, and further analysis is necessary to reveal patterns in this area. Learners used mostly Hungarian in peer–peer interactions, except for the rote-learned or prescribed dialogues to be practised. Children in both teacher-fronted and pair-work activities used English more often in controlled tasks, but even in these cases task management, applying for and providing help and clarifying problems all happened in the mother tongue. There seem to be two threads running through the data: Hungarian vernacular style was used in 'on-task' social activities, like negotiating roles, disciplining and helping one another and exchanging ideas on how to do a task. Also, there was a sub-thread to this, related to group dynamics. The target language was used mainly as the formal language variety in the actual language-focused activity, and children seemed to be aware of these distinctions.

As for how patterns of interaction changed with age, children from the very first year of the FLL experience distinguished between the institutional discourse to be accomplished in the target language, and all the rest which was perceived as manageable only in Hungarian. They used Hungarian in peer–peer interaction even when, in the upper grades, the necessary language competence would have been at their disposal; at around the age of 11 to 12, a definite decline was observed in learners' willingness to use the target language. In my view, the reasons for this phenomenon are not linguistic but social and psychological: belonging to the group is more important for learners than accommodation to classroom norm and the teacher's expectations. Communicating in Hungarian with native-speaking friends is just natural.

According to Tarone and Swain (1995), children do not use the target language as they lack the vernacular style in it. To me this seems to be one of the reasons, but more importantly, learners unconsciously indicate what is spontaneous for them, and whose expectations they wish to come up to. Communicative FL teaching materials do in fact provide input in the vernacular style, sometimes they even overemphasise this aspect. Similarly, such input is available in two-way immersion programmes, as well as in the FL context in the media.

One of the ways of integrating the language necessary for informal social interactions may be available while using negotiation in the classroom: children are involved in decision-making in various areas, they need to vote, argue for or against each others' suggestions, while using the target language for meaningful social purposes (Nikolov, 1999).

The weaknesses of this study are manifold: the classrooms were randomly chosen, and the same contexts were observed only three times; the observers were novices to the field; and no quantitative analysis of the data was conducted. As children tended to use Hungarian, data were insufficient to identify what strategies they used to modify their input for each other in the target language; most frequently they applied translation, repetitions and expansions, but it is hard to estimate how frequent or useful these strategies were in the long run. As for code-switching, all of the examples could be classified as unintentional switches, but not all of them were related to proficiency. There were many more content words than function words in the data, but statistical analysis was not possible. The teacher's role was not explored in any detail, though I hope valuable insights will be gained in further analyses.

Finally, I would like to point out some of the pedagogical implications. For me as a primary school teacher of English with extensive experience of similar children, most of the data sounded like language use that I had heard in my classes, but never had a chance to tape-record. I am shocked by how infrequently children in the corpus heard or used English, and feel worried about the possible outcomes. In such circumstances teachers have to do everything to counterbalance the lack of input. It is as if by magic that some children still develop. Or else, they must be 'natural-born speakers of English.'

Acknowledgement
This title was borrowed from Ditz and Vasvári (1996).

Appendix

Transcription conventions

The conventions are based on van Lier (1988:243-244) and are as follows:

T	teacher
P1, P2,	identified learner
PP	several learners simultaneously
/yes/yah//ok//huh?///	overlapping responses
.,..,.....,	pause; three periods approximates one second
?	rising intonation
!	strong emphasis
OK. Now.	a period indicates falling intonation
So, then	a comma indicates low-rising intonation
the:::, er:	one or more colons indicate lengthening of the preceding sound
((points to book))	double brackets indicate comment on classroom events
Igen. (Yes.)	brackets indicate translation into English of previous Hungarian utterance
Well, yes.	capitals are used both for proper names and to indicate beginnings of sentences

7 Assessment of Young Learners' English: Reasons and Means

Pauline Rea-Dickins, Shelagh Rixon
*Centre for English Language Teacher Education,
University of Warwick*

Introduction

This paper addresses a major problem in many contexts where teachers recruited to teach a foreign language (FL) – in our case English as a Foreign Language (EFL) – are experienced primary teachers in other subjects, but entirely new recruits to language teaching, or the language teachers involved are more accustomed to teaching and assessing English with older pupils in secondary schools. For the former group, issues of assessment at primary level in their own countries in subjects like Maths and History may be well understood, but the ways in which they might approach assessment of pupils in a foreign language will probably be very new. The teachers trained to teach English to secondary school pupils may need guidance in how to observe younger children, or in how to set up appropriate challenges for their younger pupils that will elicit information appropriate for decision-making in the classroom. Assessment data are presented in this paper from four sources: findings from a survey in primary EFL contexts, an exploratory school-based case study, and an analysis of some assessment procedures typically used with young primary EFL learners.

Issues of general 'good practice' will always be relevant in considering the ways in which assessment might be done, but these will often be modified by local requirements and conditions, and especially by culturally influenced views of what it is to 'know' or to be able to do something in a foreign language. Beyond the question of finding technical means to assess pupils appropriately – in the most reliable, valid and fair way – lie the issues of why assessment is actually done in a particular country or institution, to whom the results are reported, how they are reported, and what action is generated by the whole process. Our hypothesis about EYL was that assessment practices in each country would tend to follow the assessment traditions that apply for other curricular content in that country, and that these may not always be the most useful in eliciting better information on how Young Learners learn languages and on how they might be supported to do better in their language learning.

A rough-and-ready definition of school-based language assessment could be: the collection of data on language use by pupils in classroom language learning.

This might take the form of observing day-to-day oral or written performance in class or in written homework, or by setting specially designed challenges in oral or written 'tests'. The data could be analysed in a multiplicity of ways; for example, for the quantity of language that pupils have at their command, for the formal accuracy and complexity that they display in its use, and also for the quality(ies) of the communicative use to which they can put their linguistic resources.

In an ideal situation the means of assessment would be very much determined by the reasons for assessment, and by the concerns of those individuals or stakeholder groups who receive the reports on the results. In this respect we may note the variety of purposes for which EFL has been introduced into the primary curriculum (e.g. to achieve social, linguistic, and communicative competence in a language, to develop inter-cultural awareness, to reap cognitive benefits through an early start in a foreign language), and the expectation that these different aspects of 'knowing a language' might be assessed.

The research project

Since we are aware that much of the research on the implementation of assessment has been conducted in the area of adult language education (e.g. Brindley, 1995; but see Breen *et al.*, 1997 as an exception), the research reported here focuses on an investigation of teachers' and teacher trainers' experiences of, and attitudes towards, the assessment of primary EFL learners. This was done in three ways:

1 by a survey questionnaire (see note 1 on page 100);
2 by two school-based case studies as a follow up to initial responses to the survey questionnaire;
3 by the collection and analysis of assessment instruments from published sources and from those provided by teachers in our samples.

Most of the findings reported below are derived from sources 1 and 2 above.

The survey
Aims
The rationale for the survey was an attempt to get an overview of some of the key issues in relation to the implementation of assessment in primary English as a Foreign Language classes, as well as to build up a profile of teachers' subjective representations of the assessment process.

Procedure
A survey questionnaire was devised to get an overview of beliefs and practice in a range of different countries. The sampling may be described as purposive in the sense that in the course of our work with teachers, we asked them to complete, or arrange to have completed, a questionnaire.

The results reported here are based on a sample of 120 teachers and teacher trainers. The majority of respondents were from European countries, with the highest number from Italy (36.1 per cent), Hungary (27.1 per cent) and Greece (9 per cent). A few returns (7 per cent) were from non-European contexts such as South America, Indonesia and Namibia; (see Appendix for a full breakdown of the sample). Of the respondents, 63 per cent identified themselves as primary language teachers, 9 per cent as teacher trainers, with 11 per cent functioning as both teachers and teacher trainers; 17 per cent did not indicate their status.

The questionnaire was in English and was completed by most respondents in English, with the exception of some of the Italian responses, which were subsequently translated into English. Overall, there were few difficulties in understanding the responses given, which indicates that those who chose to complete our questionnaire had achieved a certain level of English language proficiency, which we regard to be somewhere between PET and FCE levels. In a survey of this kind, it is impossible to know about the ways in which our questions were actually interpreted.

Findings

The results reported here relate to the main issues identified above.

ARE YOUNG LEARNERS ASSESSED AND, IF SO, WHY?

As an overview question, we asked respondents whether they assessed their children for English in any way. The findings from our survey demonstrate overwhelmingly that children are assessed, with 93 per cent (N =114) indicating yes; only 3 per cent ticked no and a further 3 per cent chose not to answer this question. Teachers may not, however, have a choice in whether they assess their learners or not, since this may be an administrative requirement of the school, and so we also asked for views on the appropriacy of assessment in primary FL classes. Here, the majority (80 per cent) indicated that they thought primary children should be assessed, with only 5 per cent saying no; a further 15 per cent did not answer this question. The picture thus emerging from our sample is that teachers and trainers worked in contexts where primary FL learners were assessed and that they felt that it was appropriate to do so.

In order to investigate further the actual practice of assessment within the respondents' own teaching and learning contexts, they were asked the main reason *why* their children were assessed.

Table 1 Why is assessment carried out? (N=122)

To help in your teaching	87 per cent
To provide information for administrative purposes	3 per cent
To provide information to parents	2.5 per cent
As part of certification at the end of primary school	2.5 per cent
No response	5 per cent

From Table 1, it would seem that the main purpose for assessment was to inform classroom planning and action, with a few concerned with having formally to report results from assessment for administrative purposes. The formative dimension of testing was further supported by 59 per cent (of those who indicated 'to help teaching'), stating that they used tests to check on learner progress, as a diagnostic tool (5.7 per cent), and to provide feedback to learners (6 per cent). There was very little reported use of formal standardised tests. These, it is assumed, arose in connection with the 'certification' function of testing at the end of primary school.

WHAT PROCEDURES ARE IN PLACE FOR THE PREPARATION AND ADMINISTRATION OF TESTS?

By procedures, we refer here to the preparation of the assessments themselves, the marking of children's work and the keeping of learner records.

Ninety-one per cent of the teachers said that preparation of assessment was their responsibility, with only three (2.5 per cent) indicating that they did this collaboratively in a group of teachers. In only two cases (1.6 per cent) the assessments were prepared outside the school, by the equivalent of a national or local education authority. This last group refers, presumably, to the tests administered at the end of primary school. A particularly relevant question that it would be important to probe further concerns the extent to which teachers are trained to perform this important function of test construction.

The teachers also have the responsibility for marking the assessments (which turned out to be primarily in the form of pencil and paper written tests) and for keeping their learner records up to date, as shown below.

Table 2 Who is responsible for marking and keeping learner records? (N=122)

Who is responsible?	Marking %	Record Keeping %
Teacher	86	68
Teachers' Committee	2.5	6.6
Teacher & Administration	2.5	5.8
Teacher & Learner	0.8	1.6
No response	8.2	18

A decentralised pattern of testing emerges, very much under the control of the classroom teacher. It is not clear why there were so many 'no responses' in terms of marking and it would be interesting to know who, if not the teacher and the administration, kept any records. It could be the case that there is no record-keeping which, in turn, would raise other issues.

HOW ARE RESULTS REPORTED?

Respondents were asked about how results on assessments were reported and by far the majority responded that this was done in grade or in numerical terms as a score or a percentage rather than as comments on a pupil's achievement.

An obvious disadvantage of a survey questionnaire is that specific issues raised by a particular question cannot in that instance be probed. Given that the reported primary function of assessment is to inform teaching and learning (see Table 1), it would be interesting to know more about how the results

Table 3 How are results reported? (N=122)

Reporting method	Percentage
Grade	30
Score (out of 20, 10 or 5)	29.5
Percentage	24.6
Comments	11.5
No response	4.5

reported in terms of a grade, score, or percentage were actually used diagnostically in, say, planning teaching, influencing learner groupings or providing feedback to learners.

ARE RESULTS USED AND, IF SO, HOW?
Eighty-six per cent indicated that their results would be used; 6 per cent revealed that they were not used; 8 per cent did not respond.

In terms of who would see these results, parents were identified as an important stakeholder group; 42.5 per cent of respondents indicated that both children and parents would see the results of the tests. Only 2.5 per cent indicated that these would be reviewed by administrators.

The importance of obtaining information for the children's parents is a point that also comes across in the teachers' comments, in terms of what parents both want and expect:

> 'Parents also want to be informed about their child's progress.'

> 'It is important for the children and their parents to know how much they have learnt ...'

> 'In our ... system children and parents expect testing and assessment.'

> 'I think children should be assessed, giving feedback both to them and their parents.'

These data reinforce the view that comes across strongly in our findings that the results had a restricted circulation for administrators, which is consistent with the finding that the administrative function of assessment did not figure as important for this group.

TEACHERS' PERCEPTIONS OF ASSESSMENT FOR YOUNG CHILDREN
It has been taken for granted that assessment is necessary, although many primary teachers seem to rebel at the idea. This rebellion, perhaps, stems from the narrow view that assessment equals a certain type of 'paper and pencil' test more suited to older FL learners. Most teachers seem to agree that principled record-keeping is part of their responsibility, as evidenced from our survey, and we would include such procedures under the heading of assessment. In our questionnaire, we gave respondents an opportunity to comment on aspects of assessment in an open-ended question. A strong finding in our data is that of the importance of testing at primary school. A variety of reasons were put

forward for this. These also raise interesting additional dimensions on the nature of assessment.

Only three teachers in our survey questionnaire sample thought that primary learners should not be assessed, justified as follows:

> 'I think at primary school children should not be assessed. In my opinion the aim of language learning/teaching is that the children should like the language and we have to develop them in this way.'

Children should not be assessed in English:

> 'A lot of children are afraid of making mistakes and it is discouraging for them.'

> ' ... because sometimes they lose their motivation and interest in English.'

There were, however, several reservations provided in our sample about testing the younger learner. For example, some expressed the view that testing should be delayed:

> 'I believe that at the end of three years' teaching the children are able to cope with some specific questions or to organise themselves for a short dramatisation.'

> '... children should be assessed in English at the end of primary school.'

> 'In our school children aren't assessed at the age of 6 and 7 because we just motivate them and make them love the language. Children are assessed from the age of 8 which is not so good because they are sometimes disappointed about the marks and they can lose their courage for learning and mostly speaking in English.'

The motivation dimension of assessment also came across through some of the comments:

> 'It is motivating for children who realise how they are making progress.'

> 'Assessment is a kind of encouragement for future learning. It all depends on how the teacher carries it out, the characteristics of your learners; the affective side is important.'

> 'Yes, as a means of creating self-esteem, independence.'

This last comment, which begins to address the meaning of assessment in a primary context and the approach to be taken, was also raised by others:

> '...tests in primary school are often related to games ... activities which do not arouse anxiety, so they are quite different from traditional tests pupils are used to.'

> 'Children should be assessed orally and in writing too.'

> 'It would be better not to test them ... but we have to .... We must be aware (and the children too) of what we/they know but written tests are not the best. We should find other ways to check their achievement (games, orally, situations).'

The following is particularly interesting, reflecting an awareness of different FL goals:

> '... primary school children should be assessed to verify their interest to the language and culture of other countries, their skills and achievements.'

A teacher reporting on her own school wrote:

> 'First the assessment is oral, or pupils get red points. They are happy about it and this type of assessment is encouraging.'

and that testing is conducted:

> ' ... in an informal way because English in primary schools is taught in a friendly way and a formal test could condition the children's spontaneity.'

Discussion

Functions of learner assessment in primary EFL

What, then, are the perceptions of the assessment process, as reflected by the teachers' self-reports in our studies? Elsewhere (Rea-Dickins and Rixon, 1997), we identify four key dimensions to assessment at primary level – to support evaluative, administrative, formative, and certification functions. Using this classification, we observe that the different functions of assessment permeate many of the teacher quotes in our samples. This puts us in a position to compare the findings from the teachers' and trainers' general representations of the functions of assessment with those of their reported actual practice.

EVALUATIVE

It is not surprising that we did not find any examples of teacher participation in a formal programme evaluation. Nonetheless, the evaluative role of assessment was fairly pervasive through a number of teacher comments, as the following three examples show:

> ' ... it is very important for the language learner and the teacher as well. It shows the lack of knowledge, bad methods, level of the students' knowledge and the success of the teaching programme.'

> 'I think children should be assessed in English because we have to measure their knowledge. We can find out how effective the teaching method is ... It is the mirror of our teaching.'

> '... children should be assessed, given feedback both to them and their parents. It also tells the teacher about their teaching.'

ADMINISTRATIVE

The comments on teachers' implementation of assessment provide a strong indication that, amongst the teachers surveyed, the administrative requirement for testing was very limited.

FORMATIVE

Teachers reported on the importance of the formative dimension of assessment in their work. In their comments, they frequently mentioned it:

> '... and from the gaps we can find out where we should help the children more.'

> '... and the children also need a kind of feedback about their achievement in language learning.'

However, it is not clear from our data exactly how the findings from the tests were actually used in informing classroom planning and action. The data strongly suggest an awareness of the need for 'results' to feed into teaching and learning. However, it was not clear whether learner assessment as implemented in schools was an integral *part* of learning, or whether assessment was actually implemented as the means to measure the summative achievement of their learners.

CERTIFICATION

For a child, unlike an adult learner, the possession of a certificate from an international examining board can have no 'outside world' value in career or education terms. Unsurprisingly, we did not receive any comments on this aspect of assessment. There was also little mention of certification at the end of school, in the transition phase between primary and secondary education.

Whilst we have gathered evidence that suggests teacher awareness of different purposes for assessment in the primary assessment context, further analysis of the data is required to determine the extent to which these different purposes are sufficiently distinguished in the implementation of assessment.

Congruence between learning goals and assessment

Above, and elsewhere (e.g. Edelenbos and Johnstone, 1996; Gika, 1997; Rea-Dickins, 1997), the goals for introducing a FL into the primary curriculum have been documented. These are varied and, aside from the more obvious one of developing linguistic competence (i.e. a specified inventory of language items: structures and lexis), these may include broader educational and social dimensions (i.e. widening horizons and awareness of and respect for other cultures), forming a positive attitude to language learning for the future. However, and rather predictably in many ways, when it comes to the content of tests, the emphasis is on what learners have achieved in terms of language. The issue seems to be about whether children have learned specific items of language ('apprentissage'), rather than whether they have developed an awareness of the nature of the foreign language ('sensibilisation') and an ability to understand a good deal without necessarily displaying that awareness in more formal, quantifiable ways through formal tests. There are notable exceptions (see Edelenbos and Suhre, 1993; Hasselgren, 1998; Low *et al.*, 1993; Mitchell *et al.*, 1992; Nihlen, 1997). In general, however, a mismatch is frequently observed between curricular aims, pedagogy, and test content. This represents something of a challenge for EYL assessment, that is to find procedures that capture – as examples – the language awareness and the cultural and the social/communicative dimensions of language and language use.

ASSESSMENT PROCEDURES

A major focus of our investigations was on the type of assessment instruments used with the younger learner of EFL. Over the period of the research reported here, we have been able to gather together a large number of tests that are or have been used in primary FL classes. These samples were sometimes appended to the completed survey questionnaires or gathered from participants on our specialist primary courses at the University of Warwick, as well as in submissions from ministries, education authorities and schools with whom we have links.

In terms of the assessment procedures themselves, there are many points to make. As indicated above, the main means for learner assessment was the traditional 'pencil and paper' test and the majority of these were either of the 'teacher-made' variety or commercially produced, either from a textbook used or from another textbook. This latter point highlights the importance that the tests that are commercially produced should provide examples of good testing practice. There were a few examples of tests produced locally, i.c. in cases where the textbooks themselves did not provide tests. In other words, teachers want and need tests: where they are not provided they produce their own.

Rather obviously in many ways, the tests analysed do not always reflect the range of activities within a primary FL classroom; neither are they necessarily able to capture the different aspects of language use that are taught at primary level. Firstly, a significant number of tests were those which reflect a proficiency type of approach, with items that are easily scorable and many of the multiple choice variety. Secondly, these tests reflect a fairly narrow interpretation of language learning in terms of the linguistic system plus a bit of functional language use. The immediate question is: does this have to be the case? What messages about language do we convey to learners through a single sentence testing method?

In some senses the tests used did not present any surprises. The predominating content-focus of the tests was on grammar and lexis. The testing of oral skills was only mentioned by one respondent in our questionnaire survey. No one mentioned listening skills. A number of tests, especially those in the commercially produced materials, reflected dimensions of exercises that primary learners in mainstream classes have to do, for example, filling gaps, matching, drawing lines to link items that are similar.

To the above, we add insights from the case-study data gathered, which allow us to draw various conclusions from the teachers' self-reports about their testing, as the following two examples illustrate:

> 'Aspects of English to focus on in teaching ... language patterns, rhymes and songs ... speaking and listening ... less reading and writing. At the same time testing focus is grammar and vocabulary ... we do not test spontaneous speaking at all.'

> 'Aspects of English to concentrate on in the lower primary ... speaking ... communication ... encouragement to boost confidence. At the same time speaking is not really tested ... measurability is a very difficult.'

Firstly, these teachers do not test spontaneous speaking. If they do assess speaking, it is restricted to learners reciting a rehearsed dialogue. Secondly, there is little evidence of testing listening and on several occasions teachers mentioned the lack of suitable materials for this. What seemed to be happening was that the teacher-made assessments focused on what could be 'easily' tested, i.e. what is amenable to testing, as opposed to what should, desirably, be tested.

What the tests did not do was to encourage learners to create coherent text, or to demonstrate understanding at a level that operates above the level of the single sentence. In the case of reading comprehension, for example, continuous texts are relatively rare in our data as comprehension challenges. The preference seems to be for a sentence-level matching operation. Pupils might be asked to identify the correct pictures to go with sentences, but it was rare to find a picture-identification task that required information from a short text to be combined so as to reach the right answer. It might be objected that young children are not 'ready' to cope with continuous discourse, but to this objection we would propose a number of counter-claims.

If young children are really not capable when it comes to natural language use, which implies coherent discourse rather than only discrete point learning, it would indeed seem premature to introduce a foreign language to them at all. The widespread claims for children's superior language learning capacities that underlie much of the enthusiasm at official and unofficial level for introducing a FL to primary-school-aged children must therefore be based on a contradiction.

We feel, however, not only that children can cope with language above the level of the sentence, but that they should be allowed and encouraged to do so, both in teaching materials and in assessment. If they are not, they are firstly being given a very strange message about the communication systems of the speakers of this new language, and secondly they are being trained in reading and listening habits that will be most unprofitable for them when they come to more advanced levels of learning. There is an irony here: Donaldson (1978) for mother-tongue learners, and others in the EYL field (e.g. Burden and Williams 1997) have amply demonstrated the highly developed 'top-down' capacities of children in interpretation and use of language. Left to themselves children have a strong disposition to use clues from the context, work out the speakers' intentions, and use their knowledge of the world to assist them (a view corroborated by our research). When it comes to the older learner the advice of authorities such as Widdowson (1978) and Anderson and Lynch (1988) has largely been dedicated to the need to help adult learners become more effective communicators through developing this 'top down' capacity, in reaction against language teaching practices and materials that, perhaps more than the ageing process, have tended to disable it. Forcing children against their natural capacities, through the limited practices that have been shown to act against the interests of even more mature learners, seems to be something to avoid, and is generally avoided in competently written modern course books for adults.

One source of the problem could lie in the 'playing it safe' practices of authors and publishers whose work has such a big influence upon what many teachers feel to be feasible. Course books for YL vary tremendously in how they treat continuous discourse rather than isolated sentence-based work, but the tendency is on the whole to offer very little development over time. Space precludes a detailed analysis of particular course books here, but a useful project for readers of this volume would be to scrutinise a number of locally used course books and verify or disconfirm our contention that the length, and coherence, of both reading and listening experiences in many course books for YL remains low from book one to book three, and often even beyond. Where tests are provided with course books, it also has seemed true from our data that even in those books in which textual awareness is gradually developed in the materials, the test items themselves tend to take the pupils back to the sentence-by-sentence mode. Comprehension questions are of the 'match lexical clue in the question to a short chunk of text' kind that for many years has been castigated in books on basic good practice in language testing (see Heaton 1990).

The daily experience of those many teachers who favour songs and storytelling as part of their approach to teaching children shows that 'big', even if simple, texts are not beyond them. If big texts in the oral mode are feasible, how much more feasible are coherently written texts of a suitable length and interest level to maintain the pupils' attention and make the reading of them worthwhile. Research on the uptake and use of the increasing numbers of EYL readers, both fiction and non-fiction, is at an early stage, but there is enough evidence to suggest that extended reading is something that is both possible for and liked by many Young Learners (see Day and Bamford 1998).

Limitations and conclusion

In reporting our survey findings, we recognise the limitations of the research procedure we used, in particular the lack of a mechanism to follow up, through interviews, responses obtained, to double check responses given, to clarify responses, to ask for evidence to support a 'yes we do this' answer, to be able to probe for further detailed information and so forth. Notwithstanding these limitations, we have a certain confidence in the findings in terms of general trends as, in many instances, they empirically corroborate the views gained over several years in a wide variety of contexts and through working with large numbers of primary FL teachers. We justify starting our research with a survey questionnaire (we have subsequently included a qualitative and case-study approach into our research) in terms of speed of access to data and, in order to encourage busy professionals to complete our questionnaire, we inevitably used a large number of multiple-choice type items. From experience we know that this introduces a (further) potential source of unreliability in that respondents may tick one of the items supplied, even though they may not be sure what it means, or do this rather than write in an additional 'other' response.

However, the survey has been informative, as indicated above, by providing corroborative evidence for what we felt was in reality testing practice in many primary FL primary contexts. It has also highlighted some key themes and identified a number of challenges for testing FL at primary level. It seems important, therefore, to move towards an expansion of the existing range of assessment methods for Young Learners, i.e. to go beyond the 'pencil and paper' test and to explore alternative approaches such as portfolio assessment. There are also implications for including approaches that go beyond the discrete single-sentence format to engage learners in working with text and language as discourse.

At a macro level, an increased emphasis on the formative dimensions of learner assessment is also suggested, to complement the readily available perception of assessment as a summative judgement on learner performance.

The assessment of young primary FL learners represents a relatively innovative context for many. In terms, then, of innovation and implementation:
1 Teachers need to know more about assessment and testing in order to engage in these processes.
2 This requires them to understand the assessment culture in which they are working (and these will be different across countries).
3 They should have access to information about any assessments they are expected to implement.
4 If required to be involved in the marking of learner performance, or to devise their own assessment procedures, they require training for this. The implication here is for teacher training and support.

It is equally important to ensure that our teaching and learning opportunities fully embrace the goals for introducing languages into the primary classroom. There are implications here at many different levels for teachers, test writers, testing researchers, test administrators, textbook writers, and policy makers. This implies the need to try and understand better the different assessment cultures from the perspectives of the different stakeholders and to ensure that opportunities exist for these groups to develop their own understanding and skills, to facilitate their greater involvement in assessment and to equip them to make choices about how to implement it.

Acknowledgement

This article summarises some of the findings from an on-going research project on assessment in primary EFL contexts which has been supported by a grant from the Research and Teaching Development Fund, University of Warwick.

Note

If you would like to share your experiences of assessment in the primary FL class, you are invited to contact the authors for a copy of the questionnaire: c/o CELTE, University of Warwick, Coventry CV4 7AL.

Appendix

Breakdown of survey respondents

Country of Origin	Number of respondents (N)	Percentage
Italy	44	36.1
Hungary	33	27.1
Greece	11	9
Indonesia	5	4.1
Czech Lands	5	4.1
Argentina	2	1.6
Germany	2	1.6
Austria	1	0.8
Brazil	1	0.8
France	1	0.8
Russia	1	0.8
Slovakia	1	0.8
Namibia	1	0.8
Not indicated	14	11.6

Statistical Procedures

The aim of this section is to give an idea of the purposes for which different procedures mentioned in this volume have been used. Readers who wish to investigate them in more depth are referred to these useful books:

Crocker, A.C. (1969) *Statistics for the teacher or how to put figures in their place* Harmondsworth: Penguin.
Hatch, E., and Lazaraton, A. (1991) *The Research Manual: Design and Statistics for Applied Linguists* New York: Newbury House.
Robson, C. (1973) *Experiment, design and statistics in psychology* Harmondsworth: Penguin.

Crocker and Robson provide good accounts of the chi-squared procedure and most other procedures that the teacher-researcher might need to use, but it will be necessary to refer to the more advanced book, Hatch and Lazaraton, for explanations of ANOVA procedures.

ANOVA

ANOVA, or analysis of variance, procedures are used when the results for more than two groups need to be compared. (For the comparison of the results of two groups the appropriate procedure is called the t-test.) In Nesi's chapter the scores from different groups of children taking tests based on information given to them under several different conditions (differing amounts of word class and morphological information) need to be compared, so different types of ANOVA procedure are selected as appropriate. ANOVA procedures are too lengthy and complex to be easily carried out by hand, but computer packages such as SPSS (Statistical Package for the Social Sciences, SPSS Inc., Chicago) are widely available in universities and other institutions, and make ANOVA and other complex procedures manageable by individual researchers.

Chi squared

Chi squared is a means of testing the probability of whether the number of times a particular event occurs is determined purely by chance or whether an association can be made between the occurrences and one of the factors (or independent variables) built into an experiment or identified in an investigation. An example from Kolsawalla's chapter in this volume is the independent variables built into the experiment of whether key words in the 'Mrs Sticklebeck' story occurred in the rhythmic refrain or the prose section. The results are put into a table which shows the number of children who recalled any of these key words and the number of children who did not in the two different conditions. The chi-squared calculations reveal the probability of the number of children remembering and the form in which the words were heard being associated in some way. A probability of less than .05 or 5 per cent indicates that there are fewer than 5 chances in 100 that the frequency of remembering is a matter of chance. This is also expressed as $p = <.05$. The result is thus said to be significant at the 5 per cent level. A significance of 1 per cent ($p = <.01$) represents an even stronger probability that the association of the events and the independent variables is not a chance affair.

Mann-Whitney

The Mann-Whitney test is used with results in which the scores of two different groups are widely spread around the median (mid-point) scores and the researcher wishes to test whether the two groups have performed in a way which is significantly different or not. The calculation is based on ranking the scores and comparing them across the groups.

Bibliography

Allwright, D. (1988) *Observation in the language classroom* London: Longman.

Allwright, D. and Bailey, K. (1988) *An introduction to classroom research for language teachers* Cambridge: Cambridge University Press.

Anderman, G. and Rogers, M. (1997) *Words, Words, Words* Clevedon: Multilingual Matters.

Anderson, A. and Lynch, T. (1988) *Listening* Oxford: Oxford University Press.

Arnaud, P. and Bejoint, H. (1992) *Vocabulary and Applied Linguistics* Basingstoke: Macmillan.

Barton, B. and Booth, D. (1990) *Stories in the Classroom* Oxford: Heinemann Educational Press.

Barton, B. (1986) *Tell Me Another: storytelling and reading aloud at home, at school and in the community* Markham Ontario: Pembroke Publishers.

Bauer, L. and Nation, I.P. (1993) 'Word families' in *International Journal of Lexicography*, 6/4, 253-279.

Berylene, D. (1960) *Conflict Arousal and Curiosity* Maidenhead: McGraw Hill.

Breen, M., Barratt-Pugh, C., Derewianka, B., Hanse, H., Lumley, T. and Rohl, M. (1997) *Profiling ESL Children* Australia: Department of Employment, Education, Training and Youth Affairs.

Brewster, J. (1991) *What is good primary practice?* in Brumfit et al. (eds) 1991.

Brindley, G. (ed.) (1995) *Language Assessment in Action* Sydney: National Centre for Language Teaching and Research, Macquarie University.

British Council and Rixon, S. (forthcoming) *Report on a world-wide survey of EYL teaching* London: The British Council.

Brown, G. and Yule, G. (1983) *Teaching the spoken language* Cambridge: Cambridge University Press.

Brown, G., Anderson, A., Shillcock, R. and Yule, G. (1984) *Teaching talk: Strategies for production and assessment* Cambridge: Cambridge University Press.

Brown, G. (1977) *Listening to Spoken English* London: Longman.

Brumfit, C.J., Moon, J. and Tongue, R. (eds) (1991) *Teaching English to Children: from practice to principle* London: Collins.

Burden, R., and Williams, M. (1997) *Psychology in Language Teaching* Cambridge: Cambridge University Press.

Burroughs, G.E.R. (1957) *Study of the Vocabulary of Young Children* Birmingham: Educational monographs, No 1, University of Birmingham.

Burroughs, M. (1972) 'The stimulation of verbal behaviour in culturally disadvantaged three year olds', Unpublished doctoral dissertation, Michigan University, in 'Effects of a story reading programme on the vocabulary and story comprehension skills of disadvantaged pre-kindergarten students' in *Report No. 39* Kerweit, N. Centre for research on elementary and middle schools Baltimore, MD ERIC ED 313655.

Byram, M. and Morgan, C. (1994) *Teaching – and – Learning Language – and – Culture* Clevedon: Multilingual Matters.

Cameron, L. (1994) 'Organising the World: children's concepts and categories and implications for the teaching of English' in *ELT Journal*, 48/1.

Carter, R. (ed.) (1990) *Knowledge About Language And The Curriculum* London: Hodder and Stoughton.

Chaudron, C. (1988) *Second language classrooms: Research on teaching and learning* Cambridge: Cambridge University Press.

Chukovsky, K. (1971) *From Two to Five* Berkeley: University of California Press.

Clark, H.H. and Clark, E.V. (1977) *Psychology and Language: An Introduction to Psycholinguistics* New York: Harcourt Brace Jovanovitch.

Collie, J. and Slater, S. (1994) *Literature in the Language Classroom* Cambridge: Cambridge University Press.

Comeaux, P. (1981) 'Experiential possibilities for bringing children and poetry together' in *Communication Education*, 30/2, 174-179.

Cook, V. (1991) *Second Language Learning and Language Teaching* London: Edward Arnold.

Crocker, A.C. (1969) *Statistics for the teacher or how to put figures in their place* Harmondsworth: Penguin.

Crookes, G. and Gass, S. (eds) (1993) *Tasks and language learning; Integrating theory and practice* Clevedon: Multilingual Matters.

Darázs, À. (1997) 'The significance of a good relationship in the classroom', Unpublished seminar paper, Pécs: Janus Pannonius University.

Daughty, P. and Thorton, G. (1972) 'Exploring language' in 'Functions of language in educational environments' Pinnell, G., paper presented at the annual conference on language and reading, Chicago.

Day, R. (ed.) (1986) *Talking to Learn Conversation in a Second Language Acquisition* Rowley MA: Newbury House.

Day, R. R. and Bamford, J. (1998) *Extensive Reading* Cambridge: Cambridge University Press.

Dickson, P. and Cumming, A. (eds) (1996) *Profiles of Language Education in 25 Countries* Slough: National Foundation for Educational Research.

Ditz, K. and Vasvári, K. (1995) 'Natural-born speakers of English', unpublished seminar paper, Pécs: Janus Pannonius University.

Donaldson, M. (1978) *Children's Minds* London: Fontana.

Du Preez, P. (1974) 'Units of information in the acquisition of language' in *Language and Speech*, 17, 369-376.

Duff, P. (1986) 'Another look at interlanguage talk taking task to task' in Day, R. (ed.), 245-258.

Dulay, H. and Burt, M. (1974) 'Should we teach children syntax?' in *Language Learning*, 23/ 2, 245-258.

Edelenbos, P. and Johnstone, R. (eds) (1996) *Researching Language at Primary School: Some European Perspectives* London: CILT.

Edelenbos, P. and Suhre, C.J.M. (1994) 'A Comparison of Courses for English in Primary Education' in *Studies in Evaluation*, 20, 513-534.

Ellis, R. (1984) *Classroom Second Language Development* Oxford: Pergamon.

Ellis, R. (1991) *Second Language Acquisition And Second Language Pedagogy* Cleveland: Multilingual Matters.

Ellis, R. (1994) *The study of second language acquisition* Oxford: Oxford University Press.

Ferrell, C. and Nessel D. (1982) 'Effects of Storytelling: An Ancient Art For Modern Classrooms' Publications of a Word Weaving Program, a story-telling project ERIC ED 225155.

Fisher, E. (1993) 'Distinctive features of pupil-pupil classroom talk and their relationship to learning, How discursive exploration might be encouraged' in *Language and Education*, Volume 7/4, 239-257.

Flanigan, B.O. (1991) 'Peer tutoring and second language acquisition in the elementary school' in *Applied Linguistics*, 12/2, 141-158.

Fóti, N. (1995) 'Child SLA in the classroom', unpublished seminar paper, Pécs: Janus Pannonius University.

Garvie, E. (1989) *Story As Vehicle* Cleveland: Multilingual Matters.

Gika, S. (1997) 'The Context of Early Modern Foreign Language Teaching and the Teachers Involved in Spain, Italy, England and Greece', in Karavas-Doukas, K. and Rea-Dickins (eds), 204.

Gimson, A.C. (1989, Revised Edition) *An Introduction to the Pronunciation of English* London: Edward Arnold.

Giovanazzi, A. (1998) 'Coherence and continuity: first steps towards a national policy' in *Language Learning Journal*, 17, Association for Language Learning.

Görbicz, Sz. (1996) 'Peer interaction in the English class of young learners', Unpublished seminar paper, Pécs: Janus Pannonius University.

Györök, T. (1996) 'Classroom interaction among nine-year-old children', Unpublished seminar paper, Pécs: Janus Pannonius University.

Handscombe, R. J. (1969) 'The Nuffield Child Language Survey', in Stern (ed.).

Hasselgren, A. (1998) 'Assessment in the Primary Language Classroom', Paper presented at the Language Testing Forum, University of Wales, Swansea, November 20-22, 1998.

Hatch, E. and Lazaraton, A. (1991) *The Research Manual: Design and Statistics for Applied Linguists* New York: Newbury House.

Heaton, J.B. (1990) *Classroom Testing* Harlow: Longman.

Hervey, S.G.J. (1997) 'Ideology and Strategy in Translating Children's Literature' in *Forum for Modern Language Studies*, XXXIII/1, 60-72.

Herzen, A. (1994) *Childhood, Youth and Exile* Oxford: Oxford University Press.

Holderness, J. (1991) 'Activity-based teaching approaches to topic-centred work' in *Teaching English to Children* Brumfit, C., Moon, J. and Tongue, R. (eds).

Horváth, P. (1997) 'The use of the mother tongue in foreign language classrooms', unpublished thesis, Pécs: Janus Pannonius University.

Jain, M. (1981) 'On meaning in the foreign learner's dictionary' in *Applied Linguistics*, 2/1, 274-285.

Johnson, K.E. (1995) *Understanding communication in second language classrooms* Cambridge: Cambridge University Press.

Karavas-Doukas, K. and Rea-Dickins, P. (eds) (1997) *The Teaching of Foreign Languages in European Primary Schools: Evaluating Innovation and Establishing Research Priorities* University of Warwick: CELTE.

Kovács, K. (1996) 'Classroom interaction', unpublished seminar paper, Pécs: Janus Pannonius University.

Kramsch, C (1994) *Context and Culture in Language Teaching* Oxford: Oxford University Press.

Krashen, S. (1981) *Second Language Acquisition and Second Language Learning* Oxford: Pergamon.

Krashen, S. and T. Terrell (1983) *The Natural Approach* Oxford: Pergamon.

Kusz, V. (1997) 'Oral learner-learner interaction in the foreign language classroom', unpublished thesis, Pécs: Janus Pannonius University.

Kutas, R. (1997) 'An analysis of children's interaction in the classroom', unpublished seminar paper, Pécs, Janus Pannonius University.

Leclerq, J. (1969) 'The CREDIF Child Language Survey', in Stern (ed.).

Long, M. and Porter, P. (1985) 'Group work, interlanguage talk, and second language acquisition' *TESOL Quarterly*, 19/1, 115-123.

Low, L., Duffield, J., Brown, S. and Johnstone, R. (1993) *Evaluating Foreign Languages in Primary Schools* Scottish CILT, University of Stirling.

Lucas, T. and Katz. A. (1994) 'Reframing the debate: The roles of native languages in English-only programs for language minority students' in *TESOL Quarterly*, 28/3, 537-561.

Mackey, W.F. (1969) 'Trends and Research in Methods and Materials' in Stern (ed.).

Maingay, S. and Rundell, M. (1987) 'Anticipating learner's errors – Implications for dictionary writers' in Cowie, A. (ed.) *The Dictionary and the Language Learner: Papers from the EURALEX Seminar at the University of Leeds, 1-3 April 1985, Lexicographica Series Maior 17* Tübingen: Niemeyer Verlag, 128-135.

Mándy, R. (1997) 'Peer interaction in the classroom', unpublished seminar paper, Pécs: Janus Pannonius University.

Martin, J. (1972) 'Rhythmic (hierarchical) versus serial structure in speech and other behaviour' in *Psychological Review*, 79: 487-509.

McGee, K. (1983) 'Mother goose in the ESL classroom', paper presented at the Rocky Mountain Regional TESOL Conference 2nd Salt Lake City ERIC ED 238362.

McKeown, M. (1991) 'Learning word meanings from definitions: problems and potential' in Schwanenflugel, P. (ed.) *The Psychology of Word Meanings* Hillsdale, New Jersey: Lawrence Erlbaum, 137-156.

Melton, A. (1970) 'The situation with respect to the spacing of repetitions and memory' in *Journal of Verbal Learning and Verbal Behaviour*, 9, 596-606.

Merza, P. (1997) 'An analysis of children's interaction in the classroom', unpublished seminar paper, Pécs: Janus Pannonius University.

Miller, P.H. and Seier W.L. (1994) 'Strategy utilisation deficiencies in children: when, where and why' in *Advances in Child Development and Behaviour*, 25, 107-156.

Miller, G. and Gildea, P. (1985) 'How to misread a dictionary' in *AILA Bulletin*, 1985, 13-26.

Miller, G. and Gildea, P. (1987) 'How children learn words' in *Scientific American*, September 1987, 86-91.

Mitchell, E. (1983a) 'Formative assessment of reading', Working paper 20 in *Search-do reading: (2) Using a dictionary – a preliminary analysis* Aberdeen: College of Education.

Mitchell, E. (1983b) 'Formative assessment of reading', Working paper 21 in *Search-do reading: (3) Difficulties in using a dictionary* Aberdeen: College of Education.

Mitchell, R., Martin, C. and Grenfell, M. (1992) 'Evaluation of the Basingstoke Primary Schools Language Awareness Project: 1990/91', Occasional paper 7, University of Southampton, Centre for Language Education.

Mózes, É. (1995) 'First and second language use in a classroom', unpublished seminar paper, Pécs: Janus Pannonius University.

Nesi, H. (1994) 'The effect of language background and culture on productive dictionary use' in Martin, W., Meijs, W., Moerland, M., ten Pas, E., van Sterkenburg, P., and P. Vossen (eds) *Proceedings of the 6th Euralex International Congress* Amsterdam: Euralex, 577-585.

Nesi, H. and Meara, P. (1994) 'Patterns of misinterpretation in the productive use of EFL dictionary definitions' in *System*, 22/1, 1-15.

Nihlen, C. (1997) 'National Test of English for the 5th Year in Swedish Schools', Paper presented at the Euroconference on Evaluating Innovation and Establishing Research Priorities in the Teaching and Learning of Foreign Languages in European Primary Schools, University of Warwick, Coventry.

Nikolov, M. (1994) 'Perspectives on child second language acquisition in the classroom', unpublished PhD dissertation, Pécs: Janus Pannonius University.

Nikolov, M. (1999) 'We do what we like: Negotiated classroom work with Hungarian children' in Breen, M. and Littlejohn A. (eds) *The process syllabus* Cambridge: Cambridge University Press.

Nunan, D. (1989) *Designing tasks for the communicative classroom* Cambridge, Cambridge University Press.

Nunan, D. (1989) *Understanding language classrooms* London: Prentice Hall.

Parks, T. (1996) *An Italian Education* London: Secker and Warburg.

Pease-Alvarez, L. and Winsler, A. (1994) 'Cuando el maestro no habla Espanol: Children's bilingual language practices in the classroom' in *TESOL Quarterly*, 28/3, 507-535.

Pék, M. (1996) 'Research paper on pupil-pupil interaction in a primary school', unpublished seminar paper, Pécs: Janus Pannonius University.

Phillipson, R. and Skutnabb-Kangas T. (1995) 'Papers in European language policy', ROLIG-papir 53, Roskilde: Roskilde Univeritetscenter.

Pica, T., Kanagy, R. and Faludon, J. (1993) 'Choosing and using communicative tasks for second language instruction and research' in Crookes, G. and Gass, S. (eds).

Pica, T. and Doughty, C. (1985) 'Input and interaction in the communicative language classroom: A comparison of teacher-fronted and group activities' in Gass, S. and Madden, C. (eds) (1985) *Input in second language acquisition* Cambridge MA: Newbury House.

Pica, T., Lincoln-Porter, F., Papinos, D. and Linnell J. (1996) 'Language Learners' Interaction: How does it address the input, output, and feedback needs of L2 learners?' in *TESOL Quarterly*, 30/1, 59-84.

Poulisse, N. and Bongaerts, T. (1994) 'First language use in second language production', in *Applied Linguistics*, 15/1, 36-57.

Prabhu, N.S. (1992) 'The dynamics of the language lesson', in *TESOL Quarterly*, 26/2, 225-241.

Raban, B. (1988) *The spoken vocabulary of five-year old children* Reading: Reading and Language Information Centre, School of Education, University of Reading.

Rea-Dickins, P. and Rixon, S. (1997) 'The Assessment of Young Learners of English as a Foreign Language', in Clapham C. and Corson D. (eds) *Encyclopaedia of Language and Education, Volume 7: Language Testing and Assessment* Netherlands: Kluwer Academic Publishers, 151-161.

Rea-Dickins, P. and Rixon, S. (1998) 'Assessment of Young Learners' (interim report on a research project) in *English Language Teaching News*, 34, February 1998, 47-54.

Rixon, S, (1992) 'State of the art article; English and other languages for younger children: practice and theory in a rapidly changing world' in *Language Teaching*, 25/2, Cambridge University Press.

Rixon, S. (1991) 'The role of fun and games activities in teaching young learners', in Brumfit, C. *et al.* (eds).

Roach, P. (1983) *English Phonetics and Phonology* Cambridge: Cambridge University Press.

Robson, C. (1973) *Experiment, design and statistics in psychology* Harmondsworth: Penguin.

Rothkopf, E. and Coke, E. (1963) 'Repetition interval and rehearsal method in learning equivalencies from written sentences', in *Journal of Verbal Learning and Verbal Behaviour*, 2, 406-416.

Seedhouse, P (1996) 'Classroom interaction: possibilities and impossibilities' in *ELT Journal*, 50/1, 16-24.

Somlyódi, N. and Vándor, A. (1995) 'Research paper on Child SLA', unpublished seminar paper, Pécs: Janus Pannonius University.

Somogyi, B. and Baksa, G. (1995) 'Research paper on student-student interaction', unpublished seminar paper, Pécs: Janus Pannonius University.

Spolsky, B. (1989) *Conditions for second language learning* Oxford: Oxford University Press.

Stern, H.H. (ed.) (1969) *Languages and the Young School Child* Oxford: Oxford University Press.

Stewig, J. (1978) 'Story Teller: Endangered Species?' in *Language Arts*, 55/3, 339-345.

Tarone, E. and Swain, M. (1995) 'A sociolinguistic perspective on second language use in immersion classrooms' in *Modern Language Journal*, 79/2, 166-178.

Tavali, Zs (1996) 'Student-student interaction', unpublished seminar paper, Pécs: Janus Pannonius University.

Taylor, M. (1990) 'Books in the classroom and knowledge about language' in Carter, R. (ed) *Knowledge About Language And The Curriculum*.

Tóth, E (1995) 'Learner-learner interaction in the classroom', unpublished seminar paper, Pécs: Janus Pannonius University.

Travers, J. (1988) 'Tunes for Bears to Dance To', paper presented at the Annual Meeting of the TESOL 22nd, Chicago, Il ED 299799.

Trelease, J. (1982) *The Read Aloud Handbook* Harmondsworth: Penguin Books.

Vajda, E. (1997) 'Interaction in the English and Spanish foreign language classes', Unpublished seminar paper, Pécs: Janus Pannonius University.

van Lier, L. (1988) *The classroom and the language learner* London: Longman.

Wallace, M. (1982) *Teaching Vocabulary*, London: Heinemann.

Weinert, R. (1995) 'The role of formulaic language in second language acquisition: a review' in *Applied Linguistics*, 16/2.

Wells, G. (1985) *Language Development in the Pre-School years* Cambridge: Cambridge University Press.

Wells, J. (1994), 'Phonology in EFL Teaching' in Bowers, R. and Brumfit, C. (eds) *Applied Linguists and Language teaching, Review of English Language Teaching*, 2/1 Basingstoke: Modern English Publications.

Widdowson, H. (1978) *Teaching Language as Communication* Oxford: Oxford University Press.

Wierzbicka, A. (1997) *Understanding Cultures Through Their Key Words* Oxford: Oxford University Press.

Wilkins, D. (1972) *Linguistics and Language Teaching* London: Edward Arnold.

Williams, M. (1991) 'A framework for teaching English to young learners' in Brumfit *et al.* (eds).

Willis, J. (1996) *A framework for task-based learning* Harlow: Longman.

Wong-Fillmore, L. (1985) 'When does teacher talk work as input?' in Gass, S. and Madden, C. (eds) (1985) *Input in second language acquisition* Cambridge MA, Newbury House.

Wong-Fillmore, L. (1991) 'Second-language learning in children: A model of language learning in social context' in Bialystok, E. (ed.) (1991) *Language processing in bilingual children* Cambridge: Cambridge University Press.

Yule, G. (1997) *Referential Communication Tasks* Mahwah, New Jersey: Lawrence Erlbaum.

Yule, G. and Powers, M. (1994) 'Investigating the communicative outcomes of task-based interaction' in *System*, 22/1, 81-91.

Zobairi, N. and Gulley, B. (1989) 'The Told Tale: oral story telling and the young', paper presented at the annual meeting of the National Association for Education Young Children, REICH ED 319517.